101 College Admissions Essays
That Made a Difference

Nancy L. Nolan, Ph.D.

Electronic, paperback and CD versions published by:

Magnificent Milestones, Inc.
www.ivyleagueadmission.com

ISBN   9781933819440

Disclaimers:

(1) This book is a compilation of successful admission essays; it does not claim to be the definitive word on the subject of college admission. The opinions expressed are the personal observations of the author based on her own experiences. They are not intended to prejudice any party. Accordingly, the author and publisher do not accept any liability or responsibility for any loss or damage that have been caused, or alleged to have been caused, through the use of information in this book.

(2) Admission to college depends on several factors in addition to a candidate's essays (including GPA, test scores, interview and recommendation letters). The author and publisher cannot guarantee that any applicant will be admitted to any specific school or program if (s)he follows the information in this book.

Dedication

For students everywhere;
may the size of your dreams be exceeded only
by your tenacity to attain them.

Acknowledgements

I am deeply indebted to the students, professors and admissions officers who have shared their perceptions and frustrations about college application essays. This book, which was written on your behalf, would not be nearly as powerful without your generous and insightful input.

I also want to thank my colleagues at www.ivyleagueadmission.com for providing a constant source of support, along with the best editorial help in the business.

101 College Admissions Essays That Made a Difference

Table of Contents

Chapter 1: Introduction: The College Admission Process 7

  The Importance of Essays in the Admissions Decision
  Writing Tips
  Common Pitfalls
  Strengths to Highlight

Chapter 2: A Personal Experience, Life Experience, or Ethical Dilemma and its Impact on You 12

  A First / Defining Experience
  Leadership Experience
  Notable Achievements
  A Challenge You Overcame
  Ethical Dilemma

Chapter 3: An Issue of Personal, Local, National, or International Concern and its Importance to You 27

  Commitment to Political Activism
  A Change You Will Make in Your Community
  Discuss a Current Event of Particular Significance To You

Chapter 4: A Person, Fictional Character, or Creative Work that has Influenced You (and why) 40

  Personal Role Model
  Discuss a Meaningful or Inspirational Quotation
  Discuss Your Favorite Book or Character

Chapter 5: A Personal Experience that Illustrates the Diversity you will Bring to the Campus 51

  Your Unique Identity
  An International Travel Experience
  How You Will Contribute To Campus Diversity
  Your Fit for a Particular School

Chapter 6: A Topic of your Choice 69

  Childhood & Personality Development
  Musical or Artistic Passion
  Athletic Achievements
  Awards and Their Significance To You

Chapter 7: Unusual Questions from Specific Schools 83

  Discuss Your Career Goals
  Write Page 217 of Your Autobiography
  What You Wish You Had Been Asked

Chapter 8: Older & Nontraditional Students 94

Chapter 9: Addendums to Explain Unusual Situations 98

  Addendum to Explain Bad Grades
  Addendum to Explain a Low SAT Score

Chapter 10: A Second Chance: Responses to Waitlist Notices 103

Chapter 11: Final Thoughts 106

Chapter 1: Introduction: The College Admission Process

For most students, few processes are as daunting as applying to college. Competition is fierce at top universities, particularly the prestigious Ivy League programs, which receive hundreds of applications for every seat in the class. Due to the large volume of applications that they receive, most schools evaluate candidates on a two-step basis:

1. **The Numbers.** The primary screening is strictly the "numbers" that reveal your intellectual strengths. To gain admission to a specific university, your GPA and SAT scores must exceed the minimum cutoff levels that the school has imposed. Selectivity varies greatly among programs, which means that scores that are considered "great" at one school may not be competitive at another. As a general rule, successful candidates at state schools have a minimum GPA of 3.0 to 3.5 (out of a possible 4.0) and a minimum SAT score of 1800 (out of a possible 2400). At highly competitive programs, the cutoffs are as high as 3.75 and 2100 for the GPA and SAT, respectively. Candidates whose "numbers" fall below these levels can still gain admission in special circumstances, but their odds of success are greatly diminished.

2. **Personal Strengths.** Candidates whose "numbers" meet the school's expectations are further evaluated for their personal fit for their intended program. In the pre-interview stage, this "fit" is assessed from the applicant's essays and reference letters. Without exception, these documents must highlight the skills and traits that top schools covet, including honor, maturity, a solid work ethic and exemplary communication skills.

A great essay brings your "numbers" to life and provides a creative description of your performance and potential. It also provides critical information about your personality, ethics and integrity that isn't revealed anywhere else in your application. The BEST essays are short, specific and insightful. They are written by candidates who know what they want and aren't afraid to go after it.

Here is what the committee hopes to learn from your essays:

• Your unique qualifications, including the depth of your academic and extracurricular experiences

• Your personal traits and interests that aren't presented anywhere else in the application

• Your demonstrated commitment to pursuing your chosen major – and why you chose it

• How you compare to other candidates with similar aspirations

An effective admissions essay supplements the data you have provided the school about your academic and professional history, rather than simply restating or duplicating it. Ideally, it will provide the reader with critical information about your personality, ethics and goals that they couldn't uncover any other way.

The Importance of the Essay in the Admissions Decision

The most typical question we are asked about essays is how they are used in the admissions process. As a general rule, they supplement the primary admissions criteria, which are your GPA and SAT score. In highly competitive programs, the applicant pool can quickly be sorted into three categories:

a. candidates with excellent grades and test scores: good chance of admission
b. candidates who are borderline cases: the application is competitive, but not outstanding
c. candidates with low grades and disappointing test scores: poor chance of admission

Unfortunately, if you fall into category c, even a great essay may not save you from rejection. In a highly competitive applicant pool, schools usually screen out lesser qualified applicants by imposing a minimum "cutoff" for GPA and test scores. Although an essay can "explain" a disappointing academic performance, it usually cannot compensate for it. There are limits to how much leeway a school will give to a candidate who does not present a solid track record of success.

In contrast, essays from candidates in category a are usually disaster checks. These applicants have exceptional grades, test scores and impressive letters of recommendation. On paper, they are everything a top school is looking for. Their essays must confirm that positive impression.

For candidates in category a (excellent grades and test scores), a bad or mediocre essay can be extremely harmful. In a highly competitive applicant pool, each piece of the admissions puzzle (GPA, SAT score, essay, references) must "fit" together in a cohesive manner to show the committee who you are and what you have to offer. If your essay is poorly written, or reveals a lack of focus and dedication, the committee will be less likely to take a chance on you.

Surprisingly, nearly 70% of the applicant pool falls into category b, or borderline. These candidates have competitive grades and test scores, but are otherwise not distinguishable from others with similar "numbers." Their acceptance or rejection often hinges on an exceptional intrinsic quality that captures the committee's interest and makes a positive impression. In some cases, this can be their commitment to family, their dedication to community service or their ability to overcome an obstacle. A persuasive essay that discusses a candidate's passion (and how (s)he plans to use that skill in the future) can make or break his/her application; it provides the final piece of the "puzzle" that the committee needs to become excited about the applicant.

Writing Tips

In a typical day, a college admissions officer will read between 25 and 50 essays from candidates around the world. What makes a positive impression? Passion. Sincerity. Insight about yourself and the world around you.

From our experience, a great essay can take any number of forms; since no two candidates are alike, their personal statements won't be, either. Consequently, the only "magic formula" is honesty; you must have the courage to reveal your true personality, whatever that may be. Show the committee who you are and what you will bring to their program. Show them the contribution that only you can make.

We surveyed thirty admission officers on what they expect to see in college admissions essays. Here's what works:

1. **Answer the question that was asked**. If you use the Common Application, you will have your choice of essay topics. However, if you use the school's own application, you must answer the specific questions that they have selected for you. Don't play games by highjiacking the question to what you wish they had asked. Instead, follow the directions and answer each question clearly, honestly, and specifically, within the word, space, line, page, or character limit you have been given.

2. **Write naturally, but concisely**. Use simple sentences and your normal everyday vocabulary. Don't waste time on fancy introductions; get to the point quickly and reinforce it with specific examples.

3. **Use excellent grammar and punctuation**. Use logical paragraph breaks to separate your thoughts and to make the essay easier to read.

4. **Show your real personality** (let the reader get to know you). Too many essays are long, boring theoretical pieces about politics, the economy, or complex scientific concepts. No matter how well-written or researched they may be, they don't tell the reader a darn thing about the candidate. Resist the urge to recycle a class paper for your college admissions essay; it isn't what the committee is looking for. They don't want to read a rational paper that anyone could write; they want to know the unique contribution you will make to their school.

5. **Personalize your essay as much as possible**. Write about your own unique, funny, interesting experiences. Provide details to add color. Adopt a relaxed, conversational style.

6. **Use humor only if it works**. Few people can write humorous prose or recount funny experiences effectively. If you have this gift, by all means use it. Before you send out a "funny" essay, however, you should take the time to have several people read it to make sure that it comes across well on paper. Ideally, pick people who haven't already heard the story that you are trying to tell in the essay. See if they find it funny (you'd be surprised how many times the answer will be "no"). Finally, avoid anything off-color or mean-spirited, which will (however well-intentioned) reflect badly upon you.

7. **Convey a positive message** (avoid cynicism). Many applicants choose to discuss a misfortune they have experienced and how it has shaped their personality. Be very careful of your tone if you decide to tell a sad story. Avoid the "victim" perspective; instead, focus on how you overcame the situation. Show the reader how the experience helped you to demonstrate your stamina, perseverance and intelligence. If written well, these essays can show the reader that you have succeeded in the face of terrible obstacles. If written badly, you may sound plaintive, self-righteous and bitter, which will not enhance your chances.

8. **Use the active voice.** Nothing is more tedious than trying to read an essay written in the cold, detached passive voice. Although it is popular in legal and technical journals, it is pretentious and verbose in everyday writing. Keep your verbs simple and active. What's the difference?

Active Voice: The cow jumped over the moon.
Passive Voice: The moon was jumped over by the cow.

Yes, it sounds that silly when you use it, too!

9. **Explain events whenever appropriate**. Many of your accomplishments are of interest to the committee because of why you tackled them, what you thought about them and what you learned. Explain the reasoning behind your decision and how your life changed as a result of the experience.

10. **Be specific and focused.** Rather than listing several items or events, give a full description of just one. The more details you include, the more personal your essay will be.

11. **Proofread several times and get feedback from valued sources**. Explain to the reader what you hope to convey in your writing and ask them whether or not you achieved your objective. Then, accept the feedback constructively. Remember, the true test of your writing isn't what you intended to say, but what the reader actually understands. If you have totally missed the mark in your first draft, you will still have time to revise it and create a great essay.

12. **Revise and polish until it is perfect**. Give yourself enough time to do the essay justice. From our experience, successful applicants usually spend several hours deciding the correct approach, constructing an outline and writing a first draft. You may have to write and revise multiple drafts before you are satisfied with your essay. That's fine – it's all part of the process. You aren't "done" until you have a document that you are 100% happy with.

Common Pitfalls to Avoid

1. **Don't let anyone else tell you what to write**. A sad fact about admissions essays: well-meaning parents and advisors often interfere in the writing process, which tends to sabotage the candidate's chances. Use your own best judgment in choosing a topic and writing your essay. Don't let anyone else influence you. Admissions committees read thousands of essays each year and have developed a keen eye for authenticity. As a result, it's painfully obvious when a well-meaning adult has had too much of a hand in a candidate's essay.

2. **Don't oversell yourself or try too hard**. Many candidates manage to squeeze every accomplishment they've ever had into a single one-page essay, which is sarcastically called a "laundry list" in admissions circles. Others explain emphatically how much they "really, really" want to attend a particular school. Don't take such a desperate approach; just be yourself.

3. **Don't rehash information that can be found elsewhere in your application**. By the time they read your essay, the school will already have reviewed your application, which reveals your GPA, SAT scores, academic awards and honors. Consequently, there's no reason to repeat the same material in your essay. Instead, you should use the opportunity to discuss experiences that aren't revealed anywhere else. Our best recommendation? Consider your essay to be an informal interview, your exclusive "one-on-one" time with the committee. Show them why they should accept you into their academic community.

4. **Don't write a scientific or technical paper**. The essay is your opportunity to demonstrate your non-academic strengths, particularly your personality. Don't waste the chance to let the reader get to know the real you.

5. **Resist the urge to write a manipulative or argumentative essay on a controversial issue**. Every year, colleges receive hundreds of essays that discuss the horrors of nuclear proliferation and the dangers of global warming. Sadly, they don't tell the reader anything (s)he doesn't already know. If you decide to discuss a meaningful issue, do so in the context of your demonstrated commitment to change it, either through your career choice or volunteer work. Don't confuse passive idealism (or future intentions) with productive action. A demonstrated commitment to a cause is worth writing about; passive idealism is not.

6. **Don't try to explain blemishes on your record**. With rare exceptions, it is impossible to explain poor grades and test scores without sounding irresponsible or defensive. Neither will enhance your admissions chances. If you have a compelling excuse for an academic disappointment, place it in a separate addendum to your file, rather than in the body of an essay or personal statement. (Chapter 9 of this publication presents several persuasive addendums.)

7. **Don't use large, pretentious words**. Use the simplest possible language to explain your meaning precisely. Using three-dollar words to impress the committee usually backfires because it comes across as presumptuous and arrogant.

8. **Don't be boring and safe**; tell a real story! A fresh and well-written essay will enhance your credentials and differentiate you from other candidates with similar interests and grades.

9. **Don't lie or exaggerate**. Applicants seldom realize how easy it is to detect lies and half-truths in admissions essays. Don't pretend to be someone you are not. After reading your file, the committee members will have an excellent "feel" for your character. Consequently, they can easily tell when a reported event or achievement isn't consistent with the rest of your history. From our experience, lying is a fatal mistake - a single misrepresentation on your application will cause the committee to doubt all of your other assertions. Don't risk it.

10. **Don't be gimmicky**. Avoid using definitions to begin your essay. This crutch was extremely popular in the late 90's, but is now synonymous with sloppy writing. Avoid using cute or "meaningful" quotations, unless they perfectly fit the character and tone of your essay. Quotations are terrific if they are seldom used and deeply relevant to your chosen topic. All too often, though, their usage is cliche and the resulting essay is unimaginative.

11. **Don't give your essay a clever title**. Many candidates approach the essay as a creative writing assignment, rather than as the personal marketing document that it is. Sadly, as part of that mistake, they give their essays imaginative titles that have nothing to do with the actual assignment. College admissions essays do not need titles; you simply need to write the question you were asked at the top of the page, followed by your essay (which is the answer to that question).

12. **Don't play games with the word limit**. Don't use a miniscule type size or invisible border to shrink an essay to the stipulated page limit. Except in extreme circumstances, your finished essay should adhere to the maximum word, page, character or line limit imposed by each school. Ironically, from our experience, less is more. Your goal is not to write a book, but to convey your points quickly and efficiently; don't feel obligated to "fill" extra space. If given the choice between reading a 500-word essay that is long and rambling and a 380-word essay on the same topic that is concise and effective, the committee will pick the shorter essay *every time*.

Strengths to Highlight

Your essays MUST emphasize the intrinsic traits that the committee seeks in the admissions process. Due to the high ethical standards and level of critical thinking that are expected at most top universities, your character and motivation will be highly scrutinized by the selection committee. Use the essay set to sell your whole self, not just the individual pieces that you think the school wants to see.

Admissions officers seek the following traits in college applicants: motivation, maturity, enthusiasm, honesty, Independence, humor, commitment and perseverance. To whatever extent possible, you should build your essays around the achievements and experiences that have enabled you to cultivate and display these strengths. This is your only chance to sell yourself; use it for everything that it's worth.

This publication presents 101 college admissions essays that made a genuine difference in the selection process. For some readers, their content and tone may be surprising. They are seldom academic in nature, and may seem risky to candidates who feel compelled to assume a false (or misleading) persona for the committee's benefit. That's why studying the essays is so valuable - they reveal the heart and soul of each writer and demonstrate what (s)he would add to campus life.

The following collection includes essays in more than 20 different categories. Collectively, they show the many ways that candidates have presented their achievements and goals in a creative (and effective) manner. These candidates were accepted because they caught the eye (and captured the heart) of a receptive admissions officer. They have accomplished what you are trying to do. Before you put pen to paper to write your own essays, read on!

Chapter 2: A Personal Experience, Life Experience, or Ethical Dilemma and its Impact on You

The first essay topic on the Common Application is to discuss a personal (or life) experience or ethical dilemma that had a particular impact on you. By design, this question is broad and open-ended. Depending upon the level of detail that you are willing to include, you can write about almost anything. What, then, makes a good answer to this question?

First, you should pick an experience that was significant to you on a personal basis. Ideally, it should be a defining experience that helped you to demonstrate or clarify your values. Ironically, the experience does not necessarily have to be a positive one; many times, we learn the greatest life lessons from the challenges and obstacles we face.

A common sense caveat, however: if you choose to discuss a difficult experience, be sure to explain how you have learned and grown from it as a person. Your goal is not to elicit sympathy, but to position yourself as a survivor who has much to offer the college that accepts you.

Here are several successful answers to this question from candidates who were admitted to Ivy League colleges. By design, we have grouped the essays in the following sub-categories:

A First / Defining Experience
A Challenge You Overcame
Notable Achievements
Leadership Experience
Ethical Dilemma

For each essay, we have also indicated whether or not the essay was written for the Common Application or to answer a specific question for an individual college or university. (Note: If the essay was for a specific school, we have also indicated the specified length limit for the response.)

To protect the privacy of the writer, the names of all people, classes, schools, places, teams, activities, and companies have been changed.

A Defining Experience   (Common Application: 750 word limit)

Dirty, corrupt and dishonest. *A thief.* At age three, I did not understand these words because I had never experienced evil. In a split second, that completely changed – and left me with a frightening memory of childhood.

On our way home from school, I waited in the back seat of the car while my father went into the grocery store. Suddenly, an unshaven man opened the door and began to speak to me. "Hello Sweetie, your dad said I can have this." He reached to my feet where my dad kept a bag with his wallet and personal items. As the man flashed me a crooked smile, I noticed his bad breath and dirty teeth. He told me that I was good girl for waiting so patiently. Meanwhile, I didn't move an inch or say a word.

"Hey beautiful," my dad said, opening the car door moments later, "I bought your favorite candy." I held the tiny box of Hot Tamales in my lap, completely motionless. Dad immediately knew that something was wrong, because I normally laughed with joy whenever he gave me candy. When he turned to look at me in the back seat, he noticed that his bag was missing. I told him about the strange man who had claimed it while my dad was in the store.

Looking back, my blindness in this situation demonstrates the pure innocence of my childhood. In my safe, secure world, I couldn't imagine the cruel nature of a criminal, who would literally steal from a child. The ramifications of the robbery forced me to acknowledge the prevalence of evil for the first time. Sadly, my father's stolen bag had contained my family's passports and other documents for our upcoming move to Canada. Replacing them was stressful, time-consuming and costly.

Ironically, the robbery ultimately became a valuable learning experience for me. While other children presumed that strangers were their friends, I knew that trust was not universal. I also knew that my experience as a crime victim was not unique. In the future, I would inevitably encounter other people who would steal from me if they had the opportunity. To avoid being victimized, I developed a heightened awareness of the people and situations around me, which gave me a sense of security. In my heart, I knew that this type of vigilance was my key to remaining safe.

Almost fifteen years later, I still remember the day when I lost my childhood innocence. Yet I also acknowledge that the robbery was a catalyst for my maturity and growth. When he stole our money and passports, the thief forced me to face life's harsh realities. After I recovered from the shock, I realized that there are two ways to live: honestly or deceitfully. I choose honesty. Whatever I achieve through my hard work and sacrifice brings me a rightful sense of pride. A thief will never understand or enjoy that pride.

Eventually, my naivety was replaced by a sense of gratitude. Every day offers another chance for me to enjoy life, learn new things, and become a better person. Through my curiosity and ambition, I have become a strong woman who does not discourage easily. Even in the toughest situations, I take care of myself and those around me.

Honest, loyal and benevolent. *A success.* When I arrive on the Columbia campus, I will bring my hard-earned knowledge from my first eighteen years of life. In every choice I make, I will try to embody the essence of those positive values.

Our Assessment: This essay is powerful because the candidate explained the impact of the experience upon her growth and character. Rather than position herself as a victim, she became a survivor.

A Defining Experience   (Common Application: 750 word limit)

The sunny spring day started the same as many others. On my three-block walk to school, I recited the words for my final exam in German; I hoped that I would conjugate my verbs correctly. As I took my seat in our crowded classroom, I was completely unprepared for the mayhem that was about to ensue.

My parents, however, never made it to work that spring morning. As they approached the newsstand that they had worked so hard to build, they found themselves trapped in a social and political nightmare. After months of fear and uncertainty, a group of demonstrators who opposed the economic policies of Egyptian President Mubarak started several riots that the police could not control. Along with hundreds of other businesses, my family's newsstand burned to the ground. The bodega's demise claimed our primary source of income and our sense of security in our new homeland.

As I began my final in German, I did not know about the terrible calamity that had besieged my nation. The first signal was the fire alarm, which blasted loudly throughout the school. Normally, we gathered in the gymnasium during fire drills. This was different. We weren't released until 5 pm, when our parents picked us up. I waited anxiously until 7 pm, when my father finally arrived.

I will never forget the look on his anguished face. Throughout our ride, my dad was silent. I didn't learn about the riots until we reached the airport, where thousands of people were trying to flee the country. Suddenly, I was immersed in a "breaking news story," as television crews filmed the violent demonstrations against President Mubarak's regime. My mother's emotion was a startling contrast to my father's stoic exhaustion. I was devastated by her repetitive cries, "it is gone.... all gone... all we have worked so hard for... gone." Upon boarding our "emergency" plane to Greece, I learned that the riots had destroyed our family's home and business. Everything was, indeed, gone on that miserable Friday afternoon.

A year later, that frightening day remains a defining moment of my life because it made me a survivor. Like my parents, I refused to let the violence of an angry mob end my chances for a prosperous future. Upon our return to Cairo, I helped my family to rebuild their business, which required me to work 35 hours per week in addition to my school work. Many days, we had little food and no sleep, but we survived. Through this ordeal, I discovered that I possess the same drive and determination that empowered my parents to build a future for our family. Amidst the poverty, oppression and despair that surrounded us, we remained happy and self-sufficient.

After surviving the riots, I decided to learn as much as possible about Egypt's role in the global economy. Recently, I visited the United States as part of the Global Financial Leadership Conference, which included several lectures at the International Monetary Fund about the need for emergency funding in Egypt. After hearing these talks, I acknowledged the need for someone like me to work at the IMF or World Bank as an advocate for change. By doing so, I can use my skills to preserve the social and economic future of Egypt for the next generation.

My family is living proof that resiliency comes from surviving hardships. In addition to nurturing my dream, my parents also share it. Although they are strong, hard-working people, neither was able to complete a college education. By attaining my educational goals, I am pursuing a dream that will benefit my family as well as my nation. I can't change the past, but I am determined to do my part to build a better future.

Our Assessment: This essay not only discusses a life-changing experience, but explains its impact on the candidate's career choice. After reading it, the committee felt like they knew the author; they definitely had additional insight into her motivation and character.

A Defining Experience   (Common Application: 750 word limit)

Prior to December 8, 2007, my answer to this question would be quite different. Then, my "defining moments" were challenging intellectual pursuits, such as my winning presentations at national forensics meetings. Every victory helped to shape the self-motivated woman I have become. Yet, on December 8, 2007, my entire life changed, along with my answer to this question. The birth of Joshua, my younger brother, changed just about everything.

On the night of his birth, I tossed in my bed, too nervous to sleep. I worried about my mother's labor and the baby's health. What if something went wrong? Finally, when daylight came, I took the bus to school and tried to convince myself that it was just a normal day. My theology exam was a welcome respite from my recurrent concerns about my mother.

Finally, at 3 o'clock, I rushed out of school and took the city bus to Warren Memorial Hospital. As I opened the door to room 116, I was shocked by my mother's pale face, tired eyes and unkempt hair. Suddenly, I noticed something next to her: a cart with a baby in it. My little brother! I gazed into his closed eyes, noting his tiny fists, red skin and small body. My mind drifted effortlessly into a fantasy state. He didn't look human to me, more like a little monster. Was this creature really my brother? Would he ever look human?

When we brought Joshua home a few days later, I realized how radically my life had changed. I was no longer the only child, the spoiled one who thought only of herself. In a split second, I accepted the dual role of both surrogate mother and sister, and tried to set a good example for him. Despite my lack of experience, I learned how to bathe, feed, and change my brother. To my surprise, I enjoyed the happiness that Joshua brought into my life. After years of solitary pleasures, I could share my laughter and joy with him, and he could erase my blues.

With my three-hour commute to and from Xavier Academy, I seldom have a free day to call my own, much less any free cash to spare. Yet when I am miraculously blessed with both, I share them with Joshua. We go to his favorite place, McDonald's, to share a happy meal and an Oreo Blizzard. After lunch, I take him to play in the park, followed by a stop at the public library. We often tour a museum that offers free admission on Sundays, to check out the new exhibits. Regardless of the topic, Joshua is always filled with intriguing questions.

Since December 8, 2007, my life has new meaning, thanks to my beautiful Joshua. When I get stressed out about school, the thought of his face relaxes me. When I am tempted to be selfish, the thought of his feelings encourages me to share. And when I feel like a failure, the touch of his arms around my neck convinces me that I am a hero in at least one person's eyes. Wherever I go and whatever I do, I am happy if Joshua (the newborn "monster") is with me. My greatest joy is knowing that he feels the same.

Our Assessment: This essay gave the committee personal insight into the candidate's home life, which was not presented anywhere else in her application. The anecdotes about her younger brother gave her application a much-needed personal touch – and made her more memorable to the reader.

A Defining Experience   (Common Application: 750 word limit)

Call it terror, stage fright, a panic attack. By anyone's terminology, I thought I was going to die. Or maybe I simply wanted to die, rather than accept my dismal fate. Sensing a lack of oxygen in my lungs, I began to hyperventilate. Breathe, Kelly, breathe. For a split second, I wondered if this was how people felt at the moment that they "lost it."

Ironically, to an outside observer, nothing unusual was happening. The scene was a college Italian class on the day of the first oral quiz. Yet to me, a teenage girl with a paralyzing fear of public speaking, it might as well have been a national news interview. At least in that situation, Brian Williams would have bailed me out.

I sat frozen on my chair, too nervous to move, as I quietly awaited my turn. As a high school student taking classes at Rutgers University, I was desperate to feel accepted by my college peers. I stared at the Italian book in front of me, silently reciting my mini-dialogue, although I already knew the lines by heart. Yet, in the presence of these "strangers" in the room, I felt scared. What if I made a mistake? What if I embarrassed myself? What the heck was I doing there? In this talented group of students, I needed to prove myself.

Finally, the moment arrived. "Your turn." I slowly walked up the aisle as if I had the weight of the world on my shoulders. When I reached the front of the classroom, I felt the stare of my fellow students looking back at me. As adrenaline surged through my body, I perspired and blushed. "How can I do this? How can I recite something in Italian in front a bunch of college students when I'm too nervous to present a speech in front of my high school friends?"

Yet, I knew I must do it, both to get an "A" in the course and to prove myself to my classmates. So many people, including my guidance counselor and language tutor, had faith in me. Everyone I knew, especially my parents, expected me to succeed. I had to do it for them.

Finally, I took a deep breath and yelled out all the lines of my mini-dialogue, "Buona mattina. Mi diletto per parlare oggi voi, anche se sono abbastanza nervosa. Grazie per la vostra considerazione." In less than 30 seconds, it was over. I returned to my seat, accepting praise from people with whom I had never previously spoken. "Good job, Kelly." What a relief!

Looking back, I can't believe I was so paranoid about speaking in front of people. Why was I so afraid of the students in that class? They were mere mortals, just like me. Before I enrolled at Rutgers, I had managed to conceal my fear of public speaking. Suddenly, in a competitive college environment, my insecurities rose to the surface. Ironically, that terrifying oral quiz (and panic attack) made me realize how crazy and isolated I had been. Rather than take a risk, I had let my fear paralyze me, which kept me from pursuing my dreams.

These realizations led to positive changes in my life. I began to lead class discussions, assert myself in study groups, and earn better grades on oral presentations. With my newfound confidence, I became the captain of the math club and the leader of the gymnastics team. Most importantly, I began to reach out to people, which allowed me to shed my shyness. After all, my fellow students aren't monsters: with a little kindness, many have become good friends. In my Italian class, I discovered several kindred spirits in the most unlikely setting. Although I may lose touch with them at the end of this semester, I will treasure every second I spend in that classroom.

Our Assessment: This candidate gave the audience a moment-to-moment guide to her stage fright in her college Italian class. The writing was crisp, honest, and highly entertaining. Most importantly, she also answered the second half of the question, which was to explain the impact of the experience on her. The essay was well perceived.

A Defining Experience   (Common Application: 750 word limit)

In my crime-ridden neighborhood in Bensonhurst, I faced difficult situations every day. However, I always felt safe and protected because I had my grandmother taking care of me. My entire life, I heard the story about my premature birth and the accident that had killed my mother. After months in intensive care, I was healthy enough to leave the hospital and move in with my maternal grandmother. The adoption was expensive, she claimed, but the best decision she ever made.

For the first ten years of my life, we did everything together. My grandmother picked me up after school, took me out for ice cream, and to my cousins' house in the suburbs. Everything changed on September 6, 2004, two days before her 70th birthday. On that day, my grandmother suffered a stroke that completely changed our lives.

I had just started the fifth grade at a new school, where I struggled to fit in. On that difficult day, I immediately knew that something was wrong because my grandmother did not pick me up. Instead, my aunt arrived late and asked to speak to my teacher. When we got into the car, I asked, "Where is Grandma?" My aunt hesitated and said, "In the hospital." At the time, I did not understand the meaning of the word "stroke," but I knew that it was bad. In an instant, everything in my world was completely different.

First, I went to live with my Aunt Cherie and her husband Bertram at their home in the suburbs. My new environment required several adjustments. Compared to my grandmother, my aunt ruled with a firm hand. She expected immediate compliance, while my grandmother allowed me to negotiate. Sadly, during her stint in the rehab facility, I did not have a chance to visit my grandmother much. I missed her a lot and was fearful about the future.

Second, at the beginning of the next school year, I had to start over in a new place where I didn't know a soul. Without the comfort of my old teachers and friends, school became a chore rather than a pleasure. I fell behind in the sixth grade and needed extra help. By this time, I moved back to my grandmother's house to assist with her recovery. Unfortunately, things were more difficult than before. She could not drive, so we relied on another uncle for assistance.

During these struggles, my Aunt Cherie often asked me about my grades, but I did not want to talk about such a difficult subject. Finally, as my aunt became more persistent, I admitted that I needed help. With her support, I enrolled in tutoring and academic enrichment programs that boosted my grades in several subjects. She also registered me for football camp, which helped me to make friends and become more disciplined.

Through these activities, I learned to acknowledge difficult situations and to ask for help from people I trust, such as relatives, mentors, and advisors. With their input, I can develop a plan to resolve the issue and manage my fears. Since then, this approach has allowed me to stay on the path to success, regardless of the obstacles in my way. At home, at school, and on the athletic field, it has given me the strength and confidence to be a leader.

Our Assessment: This essay is short, simple, and honest, without being overly emotional or manipulative (which is why it works). The reader understands the difficulties the author faced after his grandmother's stroke. In the final paragraphs, we also learn how the candidate has applied the lessons he learned in subsequent situations. He is a survivor in every sense of the word.

Leadership Experience   (500 word limit)

At the Hunter Leadership Academy in Nepal, I was the head delegate for our 20-member team at the International Model United Nations (IMUN) competition in Prague. In this role, I was responsible for preparing and writing our team's position papers on numerous topics, which required meticulous research, organization and collaboration from the members of our group. My first roadblock was convincing my team members to start their work during our February break, which was more than six weeks before the competition. At first, they deferred because they wanted to relax with their friends and family over the winter holiday. Later, I discovered that the issue was actually one of competing priorities. Rather than "waste" their time writing their position papers, my team members preferred to focus on their term papers for our AP History and AP Economics classes, which were 50% of our overall grade. As a top student with a solid GPA, I understood the challenge of balancing both responsibilities.

To overcome this obstacle, I approached our AP Economics teacher, who was responsible for the event. We agreed on a reasonable compromise – to make our position paper for the IMUN competition part of our AP Economics grade. In subsequent weeks, we analyzed several complex topics, including alternative energy sources in Northern Europe, the evolution of microfinance in rural India, and the impact of green technologies on the polar icecap. By dividing the research and writing assignments in an equitable way, we accomplished a significant amount of work in a short period of time. Most importantly, we built a solid rapport with each other, which allowed us to collaborate effectively and improve the quality of our ideas.

During the actual event, our months of dedication and commitment paid off. The competition from other schools was formidable, but we simply refused to give up. Instead, our delegates debated strongly and insightfully on a variety of fascinating financial, political, and economic issues. Thanks to our extensive preparation and research, we had perceptive responses to all of our opponent's positions, which we delivered with maturity and confidence. Occasionally, when the competition got tense, we drew upon the solid rapport we had developed as a team; regardless of what happened, we all knew that we had 19 partners who were behind us 100%. In the end, we finished third (out of thirty-six teams) for Overall Team

Performance and I won the award as Best Delegate. When we left the competition that night, we were justifiably thrilled by our results.

Serving as the head delegate taught me several lessons in leading and motivating a high performance team. First, I recognized the importance of starting early, which allowed us to research topics in greater depth than our competitors. Second, I discovered the benefits of brainstorming ideas with my team members, who each brought a different perspective to the topics. By discussing them as a group, we were able to identify and diffuse most of our opponent's arguments. Third, I learned to ask for what I needed as a leader, which, in this case, was a creative way to free our time from the demands of our AP Economics assignment. Without our teacher's concession, we could not have balanced our graded assignments and position papers at the same time. Finally, this experience taught me to nurture and respect the talents of my peers, who valued our success in this competition as much as I did. Our subsequent victory was truly a shared event.

Our Assessment: The strength of this essay is that it explains: (1) a problem that the author solved in a creative way; (2) his ability to lead a group in stressful circumstances; and (3) what the experience meant to him as a person. The essay was not personal in nature – and it didn't need to be. Instead, it focused on leadership in a concise and effective way.

Leadership Experience (400 word limit)

During my junior year, I completed a Civics course that required us to identify a project that would enhance the school environment. In previous years, the School Board used the reports as formal business plans for campus improvements, such as a security system and free Wi-Fi access. Accordingly, our class felt considerable pressure to come up with a really great idea. For our project, we decided to revise the parking policies and structures at the school, which needed considerable improvement. Many students couldn't find parking on campus, while others parked in the faculty and staff lots without authorization. In addition, there was an imbalance in the size of the parking lots versus the number of people who were allowed to use them. In an open election, the class chose me as the leader of the project.

As the quarter winded down, we conducted a cost and benefits analysis for our proposed solution. As project leader, I coordinated the group's efforts and guided them through a final stressful weekend. When we presented our results to the school administrators, they were intrigued by our suggestion to use the abandoned football stadium for overflow parking. The land was free, readily available, and easy to access. For the cost of a few signs, the campus parking capacity could potentially increase by 150%. Our principal used our analysis to convince the school board to fund the project. Just three weeks later, the old abandoned football stadium was a heavily-used parking lot. I was proud to be associated with such a practical and beneficial project.

This project taught me how to establish goals and outline the means to achieve them. I also learned how to plan my work in order to meet a short-term deadline. Although we conducted a feasibility study in our initial planning, we were overly optimistic for the timing required for several key steps. Ultimately, we completed the project in the allotted time by pooling our resources and working as a cohesive unit. This was my first experience as a group leader and a great foundation for my future efforts as a student leader on campus.

Our Assessment: This essay was particularly challenging, due to the short length limit that the university imposed. Nevertheless, the candidate did an excellent job of explaining her role in leading an important project for her school. The essay was well perceived.

Leadership Experience (400 word limit)

Moms Unlimited is a free counseling program that I helped to create in 2006 for young, unmarried, pregnant teens in the San Francisco Bay Area. From my volunteer work as a Big Sister, I knew several girls who wanted to keep their babies, but lacked the skills to care for them. With the help of my mother (a pediatrician), I formed Moms Unlimited as a free resource for pregnant girls and their families. I raised awareness for the program by making presentations at high schools, college campuses and teen hangouts in the Bay Area. To raise money, I solicited donations from local businesses and women's groups, who were also generous with their time and expertise. After a slow start, Moms Unlimited raised $100,000 and developed a great reputation around the city. After four years of continuous growth, we have 55 volunteers and more than 300 pregnant young women participating in the program.

Moms Unlimited succeeded because it provides a valuable service to a neglected segment of society. Although most people agree (in theory) that teen mothers need emotional support, no one in the area took the initiative to develop a program that was aimed exclusively at teens. In the past three years, I have met several wonderful mothers who got a head start in life because Moms Unlimited listened to their concerns, answered their questions, and diminished their stress during difficult times. We also provided the educational resources they needed to build a successful future. As a result, many of our first clients have finished high school, enrolled in college, and become volunteers for Moms Unlimited, to share with others the lessons and skills that we taught them.

Although I started Moms Unlimited as a social resource, it eventually helped me to identify my professional calling. After college, I plan to pursue a career in social work or psychology, to combine my interest in emotional health with the delivery of practical solutions and human services. Ideally, I also plan to pursue similar entrepreneurial and volunteer opportunities in the public sector. Thus far, my commitment to Moms Unlimited has enabled me to enrich the lives of young women and their children in a unique manner. As a college student, I will share what I have learned about creating a non-profit social enterprise and its positive effect in my community.

Our Assessment: This candidate had received considerable media attention for the organization she formed, which gave her a definite edge in the admissions process. Ironically, she did not submit this essay about Moms Unlimited as her primary application essay. Instead, she wrote about her love of music, which gave the committee a chance to learn something completely new about her. Then, the candidate wrote this shorter essay in response to a university's prompt about a meaningful leadership experience. In the end, the strategy paid off – the school was highly impressed by the depth of her skills in two very different areas.

Leadership Experience (400 word limit)

Although I have always been an artist, I did not believe that I could earn a living selling hand-made necklaces or custom-designed T-shirts from the comfort of my home. A few casual visits to the flea market suggested otherwise. Here in South Florida, there is a terrific market for seashore-related items. Tourists particularly love handcrafted gifts that are decorated with seashells, animal prints, and tropical motifs. To capitalize on this theme, I started a small internet mail order business to market my custom-made belts, earrings and necklaces to a worldwide audience.

I started with just a few hundred dollars and a Saturday afternoon at our local flea market. In a single day, I sold more than one hundred sample items and reinvested all of the profits back into the business. I also developed a fully-functional web site to offer my goods online. During the past year, I have enjoyed brisk sales and identified several highly profitable product lines.

Although I started the business as a way to pursue my passion for art, I quickly learned that there was much more to running a business than handling my glue gun. To meet demand, I learned how to source inexpensive supplies, negotiate volume discounts, and handle customer questions and suggestions. On a practical basis, I also developed my time management skills by balancing the busy holiday season with my winter exam schedule. In the spring of 2010, I learned how paper-intensive my business could be when I filed my first business tax return. Although my venture is thankfully profitable, I have a long way to go before I earn my first million!

Nevertheless, I am confident that I will get there. Despite the steep learning curve, I have definitely been bitten by the "entrepreneurial bug." During my winter break, I will expand my business by making more samples, printing a glossy catalogue and soliciting interest from local wholesalers. I will also promote my work at trade shows and craft fairs, where national buyers often search for one-of-a-kind pieces. Recently, I was invited to become a moderator for a jewelry-related chat room, which will allow me to connect with additional upscale customers. Although my free time is limited, I will exhaust every possible step to achieve entrepreneurial success. At the very least, I will go to bed every night with the satisfaction that I gave it my best shot.

Our Assessment: This candidate recycled this essay for three different schools. In one case, she used it as the answer to a question about her favorite hobby. In another, she cited it as her most impressive leadership experience. And, finally, for the third school, the candidate used this essay to answer a question about expressing her creativity. By telling the story in a concise and straightforward manner, she had a draft that was sufficiently flexible to answer all three questions effectively.

Leadership Experience   (300 word limit)

As a child, I made trivial excuses to avoid working at the soup kitchen on Sunday afternoons. I would fake a fever or some sort of homework "emergency" to dodge my shift in the pantry. My father's patient response to my excuses was always the same: "You must give back to the community whatever blessings you have received." Although I didn't appreciate it as a child, my commitment to humanitarian causes is directly attributable to my father.

His altruism inspired my greatest achievement, the Learning Cove, which is a free mobile library that serves underprivileged children in rural areas. Acknowledging the world of opportunities that reading affords, I wanted to provide the gift of books to people who did not have access to a public library. We started The Learning Cove with a shoestring budget and grew it into a thriving, community enterprise. My initial role was to champion the program by soliciting donations and assistance from my fellow students. To raise enough money to buy a used van, we held numerous bake sales and fundraisers in Kansas City. We also solicited books, tapes, magazines and periodicals from individuals and businesses in the community.

To organize our donations, I worked in conjunction with my school librarian to label and bind the books and learn the Dewey decimal system. In just three months, we recruited weekly drivers for the van and volunteers to service our customers. We now make weekly runs to seven small towns on the outskirts of Kansas City and have 2,000 volumes in circulation. My personal goal is to add another thousand volumes to our "stacks" during my senior year.

Starting the program was a challenging experience that made a positive impact on the lives of hundreds of rural children. I am committed to continuing my community service work in college, both to benefit others and to honor my father's fine example.

Our Assessment: This is a great answer to a question about leadership that imposed a short word limit. By including the references to his father, this author was also able to use the same essay to answer a question about a role model. From the committee's perspective, this answer was memorable because of the level of initiative that the candidate took and the impact it had on the entire community. It demonstrated the applicant's generosity and social awareness in a concrete way.

Notable Achievements   (Common Application: 750 word limit)

Every summer for the past three years, I have volunteered as a counselor and activities director at the Shawnee Mission Summer Camp for disabled children. Most of the participants have Down's syndrome, although a few have Cerebral Palsy, spina bifida, MS and other degenerative diseases. For six weeks, this eclectic group of thirty children (age 6 -18) learns how to swim, camp, ride bicycles, hike and attend social functions with the help of the staff and counselors. These challenging activities are a nice contrast to the academic classes and physical therapy sessions that fill the rest of the children's time.

On my first day, my task was innocuous - to take six little boys swimming at the pool. Unfortunately, I had little experience with children – and all of them needed my assistance with basic tasks, such as opening doors, getting into (and out of) their wheel chairs and negotiating stairs. I nearly froze when ten-year-old Eric asked me for help on the diving board, where one false move could have caused him to fall. Fortunately, his faith in me proved to be well placed. After a rough start, we enjoyed a fun day splashing around and playing Marco Polo in the oversized pool.

After a good night's sleep, I returned to the camp the next day with a heightened sense of confidence. To my surprise, all six of my kids surrounded the bus the moment it arrived. They were so eager to return to the pool that they had even skipped breakfast! As the summer wore on, I became much more relaxed around my fun-loving group of six. I originally feared that we would have nothing to talk about, but I really sold this group short. Although they didn't discuss quantum physics with me, they made insightful observations about everything and everyone they knew. They also shared poignant revelations about their families, hometowns, teachers, and schools. Through our talks, I learned about the children's passions, frustrations, and hopes for the future. And I was honored to be Eric's official childhood crush, although I sweetly declined his proposal of marriage.

When the summer session ended, I felt like a new person. I hadn't read or studied anything all summer, yet I felt that I had learned something that would fundamentally change my life. At school, my popularity depended upon my performance as a student and my accomplishments on the athletic field. However, at Shawnee Mission Summer Camp, I made real friends who cherished me for what I was inside, not for my achievements and potential. It warmed my heart in ways I never dreamed possible.

Understandably, I carried these changes with me when I returned to school that fall. Although I continued to attack my classes with gusto, I also spent considerable time building friendships with my peers. Over time, these connections allowed me to increase my self-confidence. If I made a mistake or gave the wrong answer in class, I wasn't ashamed or self-conscious. After my rewarding summer in Shawnee Mission, I knew that the journey to academic success was far more important than the destination. This was a huge revelation for someone who had been a shy bookworm with impossibly high standards!

The following summer brought many changes to my life, including our move to downtown Wichita. At first, my mother worried that I would "waste" the entire summer at the lake or mall. Not a chance. I was committed to spending my summer with my six best friends in Shawnee Mission, who taught me that being smart isn't about grades, being disabled isn't about physical limitations, and that being a friend means loosening up and helping someone other than myself. Eric and his gang taught me how to be a real friend and how to have real fun, which is something no science or math book could ever teach me.

Our Assessment: This candidate was a math and science whiz with a long list of awards for her analytical accomplishments. As a result, it was refreshing for the committee to learn about another side of her personality – and how she cultivated it. This essay about her work at the summer camp showed the candidate's maturity and versatility in a highly creative way. Ultimately, it allowed her to stand out in an applicant pool of other math and science whizzes who did not have comparable breadth.

Notable Achievement   (500 word limit)

When I reflect upon the events of June 11, 2008, I relive the day's emotions: my palms sweat, my heart accelerates, and all of the moisture seeps from my mouth. As my parents checked us onto Flight 311, I watched the people bustling around me, shoving through lines and scurrying toward their gates. Their grinning faces were a startling contrast to my youthful trepidation. Unlike my fellow travelers, I perceived my boarding pass as a one way ticket to solitude. As the days with my family flew by, I clung to my mother like a dieter to a doughnut, not wanting her to vanish. Yet, like the doughnut, the comforting sweetness eventually melted away. Alone in Los Angeles, I felt invisible in my unfamiliar surroundings.

A friendly child, I developed an increasing sense of shyness with each new change in school. My 'group' in high school served as a comfort zone that I could not imagine living without. Moping in my dorm room, I began to nag at myself, *"What were you thinking, flying across the country to spend the summer at UCLA… alone? You don't even know how to cook or iron!"* I was ready to cry when a sudden kick of determination steeled my spine. *I will make this a good experience.* My summer would not be hindered by something as trivial as shyness.

Buoyed by my newfound determination, I left my room and immediately caught sight of two girls. Sending up a quick prayer, I sauntered behind them and hesitantly spouted, "Hi, I'm Alicia! I'm heading to the Student Union…wanna come?" As my jumbled invitation registered in their minds, my anxiety heightened. Just as I was about to flee, the redhead replied with an accepting grin, "Yeah, that would be fun. My name's Kelly and this is my roommate, Lea." That one simple statement was my salvation, which restored my fledgling confidence. In a split second, my anxiety melted away and I began to enjoy my new friends.

Fun summer experiences quickly filled my memory bank: clutching a latte in an oversized lecture hall, giggling endlessly with Lea and Kelly in the dorm each night, and practicing the cello for endless hours until the conductor felt we had "finally gotten it right." Thousands of moments eventually culminated in a depressing scene: me, standing dejected at LAX's security checkpoint, ready to fly home to Charleston. Ironically, the eyes that once cried for my parents were now puffy from missing my friends in California.

Throughout my wait at check-in, I bid a bittersweet goodbye to my summer home. Riddled with sadness, I tripped on the tarmac and spilled the contents of my carry-on bag. As I stared blankly at the mess before me, empathetic onlookers quickly came to help. The contents on the ground reflected my dejected spirit: out of order, torn into pieces. When I reflect upon my emotional goodbye, I wonder how different this summer would have been had I not taken Flight 311 to Los Angeles. Without a doubt, my momentary embarrassment at the airport was a small price to pay for my cherished summer memories at UCLA.

<u>Our Assessment</u>: This essay is honest, detailed, and amazingly well-written. The candidate has a strong voice and the ability to present everyday moments in a memorable way. On a practical basis, this essay is also quite versatile – the author also used it to answer school-specific questions about a growth experience, international travel, and overcoming an obstacle. It was well perceived.

Notable Achievement (Common Application: 750 word limit)

My most notable achievement was surviving the 2008 National Junior Olympics, which was *supposed* to be the crowning glory of my athletic career. Beforehand, I had competed in several regional track meets, in which I usually placed first in the 440 and 880 meter runs. Consequently, I was delighted when my coach announced that I had qualified for the national finals for the Junior Olympics. Mr. Grayson beamed when he gave me the news. After winning the event in 1974, he had always hoped to sponsor a student, but he knew it wasn't likely. With a student body of just 300, the odds of finding a short-distance sprinter at Bayside High were slim, yet Mr. Grayson and I had miraculously found each other.

Every day after school, he offered me different training techniques to improve my speed and stamina. I appreciated the one-on-one coaching and really wanted to win. Beforehand, I had been so intimidated by the Olympic experience that I didn't consider myself a frontrunner. After all, I faced formidable competition in the race, including a national finalist from the previous year. Over time, however, I dismissed my trepidation and let my heart roam free. And when I did, I began to think I could win.

That feeling evaporated three days before the race, during an after-school training session. As I finished my warm-up exercises, I felt an excruciating pain in my right shin. I stumbled for a moment, then suddenly dropped to the ground. The pain was agonizing. I curled into a ball and tried to massage my leg, not knowing what had actually happened.

When I opened my eyes, I saw Mr. Grayson and three members of the boys track team running in my direction. They quickly explained the source of my injury. In a moment of confusion, my classmate Joe had haphazardly thrown the javelin in the wrong direction. He realized a split later that I was in the path of his wild trajectory, but it was too late for a verbal warning. The javelin hit me at warp speed and sliced a quarter inch of flesh from my right shin.

The emergency personnel stitched my leg in no time. Armed with pain medication, I went home to recover, amid my family's half-hearted assurances that there would be another chance next year. Mr. Grayson also told me the same thing, although I knew that he didn't mean it. By the time my grandparents called that night, I was convinced that I would scream if I ever heard it the expression "next year" ever again. I couldn't even imagine next year, or tomorrow for that matter, if I couldn't be in the National Junior Olympics. Eventually, I fell asleep in a codeine-induced haze.

When I got up the next day, I refused to accept the verdict; I was determined to complete the race if I had to crawl across the finish line. Without medical clearance, I began to sprint that afternoon. The pain was excruciating, but I worked through it. *I had to*. After years of sweat, training, and perseverance, I owed it to myself, Mr. Grayson, and my school to give it my best shot.

I would love to end this essay by announcing that I won a medal in the National Junior Olympics. Unfortunately, that wouldn't be true, and it would diminish the achievements of the talented athletes who won their respective events. But I competed in that race, although it took me nearly double my normal time. I didn't come close to winning a medal, but I won the most daunting battle of my life. I endured an injury at the worse possible moment with grace and maturity. I forgave Joe for his reckless javelin throw and didn't blame him for my injury. Most importantly, I refused to back down from a commitment, even though there would be no medals or glory in the end. Thus, although I wasn't a winner in the classic sense, I honestly feel that the races were my finest hour. As for winning the National Junior Olympics, there's always next year.

<u>Our Assessment</u>: Many candidates write about their athletic achievements, but few are willing to discuss a situation that did not have a happy ending. This applicant took the risk and produced an honest, touching, and memorable essay that showed his maturity and character. In the end, it differentiated him from several other candidates with similar credentials.

Notable Achievement   (Common Application: 750 word limit)

Growing up on a large farm in rural Kansas, I have always yearned to see the city. Not the mid-sized, mall-ridden Topeka, but the huge, thriving East Coast metropolis where celebrities roam, television shows are filmed, and no one ever sleeps. From the first time I heard Frank Sinatra's devotional ballad about it, New York City has been my obsession.

Ironically, although I had never been to NYC, I had managed to collect every imaginable type of Big Apple memorabilia. I ordered items from mail order catalogs, requested free samples, and extorted souvenirs from every lucky soul I knew who had ever visited the city. My mom believes that I have the largest and most valuable collection of NYC hotel bath soaps in the mid-west. Last year, she threatened to hide my *Late Night with David Letterman* t-shirt if I wore it one more time. I think you get the point: I'm obsessed.

When I was 14, I set a goal of visiting NYC before my 16th birthday. I knew that I would have to be creative, since the chances of getting my family to take me there were slim. But, to my surprise, my parents made me an intriguing offer: if I could teach one of the pigs on our farm a trick that was worthy of being selected by David Letterman's show, they would accompany me to the Big Apple. I was thunderstruck. I didn't know my parents had ever watched Letterman, much less his "Stupid Pet Tricks." Yet, I accepted the challenge, certain that I could train Spunk, our smartest 300-lb pig, to do something entertaining.

You really can't define the word "frustrating" until you've tried to train a pig. Spunk easily mastered his required tasks of eating and sleeping, but he resisted all attempts at higher education. I tried every day for a week to get him to do simple things like chase a rabbit, dance to music, or fetch a ball. It was hopeless. He stood silently during my efforts, viewing me with the amused tolerance that one usually reserves for a small child. I began to wonder if the hog I saw on Letterman tapping along to bluegrass music was a fraud.

After a month of futility, I was ready to concede defeat. Spunk was simply not going to learn a new trick to impress David Letterman. Then, as I left for school one morning, I noticed that he swirled his tail around in circles as the school bus honked its horn. Cute, I thought. He's saying "hi" to the driver, Mr. Bass. After boarding the bus, I turned around to look at Spunk and noticed that he hadn't stopped swirling his tail. Every time the horn blasted, he did it. I sensed the possibility!

I began to work with Spunk on his new trick. I would blow on my dad's old French horn (which sounded just like the school bus) and reward him for the tail swirl. It worked every time! After a few hours of practice, my parents videotaped our sessions and sent the tape to David Letterman. We received word of our acceptance just two months later. Spunk and I were going to be stars!

I won't bore you with the details of the trip and the hassle of taking a 300-lb pig to NYC. I won't even complain that Spunk's performance on the show was erratic and that he only twirled his tail 75% of the time, rather than his usual 100%. We certainly don't need to discuss my mother's reaction to the crowds, pollution, noise and rowdiness. The important thing was that we went on the show, we didn't choke, and we got a great laugh from the audience. I could have done without Letterman's "corn-fed" description of us, but I attributed it to his awkward attempt at bonding.

NYC was everything I had imagined and more. I loved the shows, the restaurants, and the historic old buildings. During our three days in town, I visited every tourist trap and attended every television taping I could find. I also filled my purse, camera bag, and suitcase with every freebie I could get my hands on. After a lifetime of dreaming, I was determined to make the most of my NYC fantasy.

In hindsight, my achievement was not actually going to NYC but in fulfilling the dream. It was the first time I had set a goal and developed a reasonable plan to achieve it. In fact, I suspected all along that this "greater good" was the reason my parents had supported the plan. They wanted to help me achieve my dreams, even if they were very different (and far away) from their own.

Our Assessment: In the first chapter of this book, we advised you to write an essay that "tells a story." This essay is one of the best examples of a "story essay" that we've ever seen. It is fun, lighthearted, and well written, albeit extremely simple in style. The candidate wrote from the heart, which made it incredibly special and memorable. As an added bonus, the applicant included a video link to her appearance on Letterman, which allowed the committee to confirm her story and see her in action. She was even more delightful in person than she was on paper.

Notable Achievement   (300 word limit)

In the winter of 2007, I was selected from a group of 300 musicians to play lead trumpet for the Ohio All-State Jazz Band. This honor, which was a seemingly impossible goal, was the culmination of many years of dedication and practice. As an adolescent, I worked dozens of odd jobs and scrounged every dollar I could find to pay for music lessons. Despite my parents' insistence that I focus on my schoolwork, I was determined to gain acceptance into this prestigious ensemble.

In retrospect, the achievement was particularly memorable because I had been rejected from the All-State Jazz Band the previous year. Rather than become discouraged, I took twice as many lessons and intensified my practice. For the first time in my life, I acknowledged the importance of setting goals, believing in myself, and persisting in the face of opposition. Today, whenever I get discouraged, I remember the lesson I learned while practicing for the audition; if I put my mind to it, I can accomplish anything.

Creatively, the event was the first time that I successfully combined my musical talents with technology. Unable to afford a professional recording studio, I used Jam Around software and amateur "home-studio" recording techniques to record and mix a dozen tracks. With my limited experience, I relied on the user's guide for the software and the support of my teacher to put together a successful audition tape. To my surprise, I discovered that I enjoyed the technical aspects of the project nearly as much as I enjoyed playing the trumpet.

Making the All-State Jazz Band was a turning point in my life, which played a critical role in defining my career path. To learn more about music technology, I plan to pursue a B.S. in Information Systems to develop a thorough understanding of the field. After high school, I also plan to continue playing the trumpet as part of Thumpers, which is a local jazz band. When I envision my professional future, I am eager to explore innovative ways to combine music and technology in my own entrepreneurial venture. Thanks to my success in preparing for the All-State Jazz Band, I am certain that I possess the tenacity to bring my dream to fruition.

<u>Our Assessment</u>: This essay is effective because it explains how the achievement influenced the candidate's choice of major (and career). It also allowed him to elaborate on his technical background, which was the topic of his primary essay. By complementing that material without duplicating it, the candidate showed the committee his versatility as a musician and computer specialist.

Discuss a Challenge You Overcame   (500 word limit)

Throughout my childhood, my struggle with obesity caused long-term damage to my health and psyche. Unlike other girls, I was never fit enough to play sports or try out for fun activities like cheerleading. Even worse, I endured cruel taunts from the bullies at school, who saw my weight as an easy flaw to criticize. Although I tried to pretend that it didn't matter, I was devastated by my unattractive appearance and the rejection of my classmates.

At age twelve, I finally took the initiative to lose weight and fulfill my athletic potential. Unfortunately, after years of teasing, I ignored my family's suggestion that I take a slow and steady approach to this goal. Instead, I dropped 50 pounds in less than three months, which was nearly one-third of my body weight. Although I was often weak with hunger, I exercised religiously to accelerate my results. My ability to maintain such a rigid lifestyle soon became a considerable source of pride.

In hindsight, my starvation diet was a dangerous way to achieve my goal. Nevertheless, I ignored the naysayers and simply focused on the numbers on the scale. Unfortunately, after a lifetime of struggle, I had lost my ability to see myself objectively. When I looked in the mirror, my 90-pound frame still seemed "too heavy" to me. So, I continued to starve myself to prevent the weight from returning.

Everything changed during a trip to Chicago, when I tried on a gown for my aunt's wedding. Suddenly, in the middle of the fitting room, my family and friends viewed my scrawny body – and they were stunned by what they saw. My arms were as thin as twigs and my bones protruded along the length of my back. As she handed me the gown, the bridal consultant jokingly asked my mom, "Don't you feed this girl?"

In an instant, I realized that I had gone too far in my efforts to be thin. When I returned to California, I adopted a sensible diet and exercise program. Most importantly, I realized that I needed to regain nearly 20 pounds in order to be healthy. With the help of a therapist and a local support group, I have maintained my goal weight for two years and attained the best physical shape of my life. Ironically, I might never have accomplished this feat without that embarrassing experience in the fitting room.

My personal experience with body dysmorphia has made me more sensitive to those who face similar battles to maintain a healthy weight and feel good about their appearance. As part of my recovery, I reach out to people who seek the support of someone who has been there – and come back even stronger.

Our Assessment: This is an honest essay about a common problem that few candidates have the confidence to write about. The candidate's ability to overcome her battle with body dysmorphia and reach out to other people with the same problem was an inspiration to the admissions committee.

Discuss a Challenge You Overcame   (300 word limit)

In 2010, a devastating earthquake destroyed my family's village in Haiti and claimed the lives of thousands of people, including my beloved grandmother. A few days later, I joined the efforts of a medical team from San Francisco that provided care and support for hundreds of injured survivors. At first, I was overwhelmed by the effects of this natural disaster, which destroyed the infrastructure of one of the region's poorest communities. As a result, many families lost the only possessions they owned, along with their hope for a secure future.

Our first challenge was to assess the area and establish a base of operations. Once we did, we served a steady stream of people who had suffered a wide range of physical and emotional injuries. In some cases, their conditions were serious enough to require immediate surgery. Other times, we treated wounds and scratches that had become infected due to lack of clean water and antibiotics. The hardest cases were the children we treated, who were grieving the loss of their entire families. Although I spoke fluent English, French and Creole, which are the primary languages on the island, I struggled to find the appropriate words to comfort them during such a devastating time in their lives.

Compared to hospitals in the US, our makeshift clinic in Haiti was downright primitive. Nevertheless, with the support of the medical team, I worked tirelessly to give our patients the compassionate care they deserved. When I returned to the US, I was deeply grateful for my many blessings, including a safe home, a good education, and the support of a loving family. Most importantly, I cherished the opportunity to use my skills to help the survivors of this unprecedented natural disaster. As part of my medical career, I hope to support additional humanitarian missions, to share my expertise with others who have not been similarly blessed. To me, this is the true spirit of medicine.

Our Assessment: Due to his EMT training, this candidate had significant medical experience to offer the relief group in Haiti, where he was born and raised. His account of the earthquake was a short and powerful essay that explained his interest in a medical career. It was well perceived.

Discuss a Challenge You Overcame   (500 word limit)

My grandmother often recited a beautiful phrase that I apply to my life on a daily basis: "O Great Eagle, do not fear the opposing storm; its only purpose is to lift you higher." These powerful words continually help me conquer life's most difficult challenges.

My own greatest challenge was integrating my Middle Eastern religion and culture into my daily life in Tennessee. As a high school freshman, the task seemed overwhelming. How could I understand and appreciate my Syrian roots when I was surrounded by a dramatically different culture? And how could I thrive in my new environment yet retain the precious traditions that my family held dear?

Despite the enormity of these questions, I was determined to find the answers. My initial interest was strictly personal: I wanted to explore my history and culture for my own spiritual well-being. With the help of two friends, I started a religious youth group at Shaker Hill Academy to educate others about our traditions and diminish their prejudice and misconceptions. To my surprise, I discovered that my own group of friends from Syria suffered similar prejudices and ignorance toward others. Although we co-existed on campus, we were woefully ignorant of each other's core beliefs. This revelation startled me and changed the focus of my group. Our mission became a two-way communication of ideas, which provided everyone with the opportunity to learn about the history, culture and religious beliefs of different groups. During my final year as

Shaker Hill Academy, I helped to organize two religious conferences on campus and the first Inclusive Spiritual Awareness Week. These events were more successful than I ever imagined.

Part of my religious doctrine is a dedication to helping others. Following my success at school, I reached out to troubled youth in my community, including those who are immersed in drugs and gangs. At the local YMCA, we organized a basketball tournament, which was a fun way to get together in a disciplined environment. As the kids enjoyed the game, they forgot about the dangers in their neighborhoods. They also enjoyed the attention and advice from successful high school students, who showed them an alternative to the risky life on the street. Our group eventually organized a youth violence conference that explained non-violent methods to resolve conflict.

The rewarding leadership experiences allowed me to fulfill a potential of which I was initially unaware. Although my original goal was to learn about my own culture, my focus quickly expanded to include a tremendous number of people in my community. My work at school helped to lift the prejudices of others who do not belong to my particular faith. I also discovered my passion for helping troubled teens avoid dangerous situations. In essence, I helped to create a forum through which people of all ages, races and beliefs can learn and grow.

In many ways, I have become the eagle in my grandmother's phrase. Each challenge that I overcome makes me stronger and better able to deal with greater issues. As I mature, I am committed to using my skills to help other people navigate similar obstacles. The stronger I become, the greater the contribution I can make. As I weather difficult storms, like the great eagle, I will be lifter higher and higher.

Our Assessment: This essay impressed us because of the candidate's honesty. Initially, in his effort to assimilate, he focused his energy on promoting the merit of his own religion and heritage. Eventually, he realized that he (and his Syrian friends) had little understanding of other cultures and beliefs. The candidate's subsequent efforts to overcome this hurdle and reach out to others truly broadened him as a person. In the end, it made him a strong leader who earned the trust and respect of a highly diverse group of people.

An Ethical Dilemma   (250 word limit)

During my junior year at Philips Academy, I roomed with a friend I had known since kindergarten. At the beginning of our second semester, Shawn began to exhibit erratic behavior. Every weekend, he drank excessively and did not return until the next morning. On several occasions, Shawn bragged about his activities, which included the use of alcohol and illegal drugs. Not surprisingly, as his grades began to slip, Shawn became increasingly withdrawn from his family and friends.

At first, I felt powerless to help him. Finally, after Shawn was arrested for possession of cannabis, I refused to remain silent. With the support of two friends on the rugby team, I staged an intervention in our dorm room, where we confronted Shawn about his self-destructive behavior. One by one, we expressed our concern for his welfare and our willingness to help him recover.

Unfortunately, Shawn resented our efforts and refused to acknowledge his problem. In subsequent weeks, he continued to withdraw from us and to drink excessively. Eventually, he flunked out of Philips Academy and accepted a job at a fast food restaurant in our hometown. Our friendship, which had literally begun in the sandbox, was permanently damaged.

This experience gave me painful insight into the power of addiction. On a personal basis, it confirmed my decision to abstain from drinking and drugs. On a professional basis, it also demonstrated what I will eventually encounter in my career as a physician, when patients ignore my advice in favor of self-destructive habits. Despite the frustration and disappointment, I will continue to try to help them.

Our Assessment: The ethical dilemma question is hard for most candidates, because they must choose a topic in which they honored their conscience and made the "correct" choice. Sometimes, those situations are too difficult or personal to talk about. Other times, the word limit is too short to really tell the story effectively. This author presented his dilemma in an effective way without exceeding the length limit. Although he and Shawn did not enjoy a happy ending, the candidate made a genuine effort to help his friend turn his life around. The rest was beyond his control.

An Ethical Dilemma   (400 word limit)

At age six, I discovered that I was adopted. I also learned that I was a welcome gift to my loving parents, who had waited for several years to receive a healthy baby. Since then, I have always viewed adoption as a miraculous process that made the three of us a family.

In the same vein, I tend to have a negative view of abortion. At seventeen, I re-evaluated my perspective when my younger cousin unexpectedly became pregnant. To my surprise, she called me one evening and confided that she was thinking about having an abortion. My initial instinct was to tell her not to do it. However, I did not want to turn my cousin away when she desperately needed my acceptance and support.

During our conversation, I discovered the many factors that would influence her decision, including money, jobs, timing, and commitment. Although she loved her boyfriend, neither was prepared to raise and nurture a child. Finally, when I asked her about the possibility of adoption, my cousin quickly dismissed the idea. Once she saw the baby, she would never be able to give it away. My heart sank when I heard those words, because I knew that they were probably true.

In the end, I helped my cousin to evaluate the pros and cons of each option. When she asked my opinion, I told her that every choice had benefits and pitfalls. Although abortions are tragic, it is also tragic when children are abused by parents who are not ready or able to take care of them. Ultimately, she had to make the best decision on her own behalf, with no outside pressure.

This situation forced me to acknowledge my bias against abortion, which was stronger than I had imagined. Looking back, I am proud that I could set those feelings aside and offer unconditional support to my cousin. I also recognized that life presents everyone with situations that have no "easy" or obvious answers, because each alternative presents its own difficulties and tradeoffs. Rather than force my opinion on others, I will keep an open mind and allow them to make an informed choice that honors their individual needs. And, in return, I hope that they will offer me the same courtesy.

<u>Our Assessment</u>: This is a lovely essay on a highly controversial topic. The candidate handled it in a mature and loving way, without compromising her own feelings. She also provided unconditional support to her cousin during a difficult time, which was not the easiest thing to do. We have rarely seen this topic presented so honestly and objectively.

Chapter 3: An Issue of Personal, Local, National, or International Concern and its Importance to You

The second essay topic on the Common Application is to discuss an issue of personal, local, national, or international concern and its importance to you. By design, this question is broad and open-ended. Depending upon your personal involvement with the issue that you choose – and the level of detail that you are willing to include, you can write about almost anything. What, then, makes a good answer to this question?

First, you should pick an issue that is significant to you on a personal basis. Ideally, it should be something that you not only think about, but have taken the time to work on. For example, everyone (theoretically) opposes drunk driving, but only a select few will join advocacy groups such as Students Against Drunk Driving. Likewise, many people talk about improving the environment, but few participate in programs to clean the beach, recycle old goods, or organize fundraisers for green-related causes. In this essay, you need to demonstrate more than passive idealism; instead, choose a problem that you cared enough to *solve*.

Second, do not ignore the second half of the question, which is to explain why this issue is important to you. If you (or someone you know) suffered a loss because of an issue, how did it affect you – and how did you overcome that setback? And what have you done since then to prevent similar obstacles in the future? If written honestly and intelligently, these essays can reveal a level of depth and insight that the committee would never learn about any other way.

A common sense caveat, however: if you choose to discuss a difficult experience, be sure to explain how you have learned and grown from it as a person. Your goal is not to elicit sympathy, but to position yourself as a survivor who has much to offer whatever college accepts you.

Here are several successful answers to this question from candidates who were admitted to Ivy League colleges. By design, we have grouped the essays in the following sub-categories:

Commitment to Political Activism
A Change You Will Make in Your Community
Discuss a Current Event of Particular Significance To You

For each essay, we have also indicated whether or not the essay was written for the Common Application or to answer a specific question on the application for an individual college or university. (Note: If the essay was for a specific school, we have also indicated the specified length limit for the response.)

To protect the privacy of the writer, the names of all people, classes, schools, places, teams, activities, and companies have been changed.

Political Activism   **(500 word limit)**

An unexpected consequence of the September 11 terrorist attacks was the discouragement of political discourse. Unlike the free-thinking 60's and 70's, when debate was actively encouraged, our current administration is quick to label any dissenters of the war in Iraq as "unpatriotic" or "soft on terror." As a teenager coming of age in a post-9/11 world, I became frustrated by a pervasive sense of disempowerment. As a result, I decided to keep the President abreast of the political thoughts of at least one dissenting voice.

Each morning, I log into my homepage at www.cnn.com, which provides the latest headlines for U.S. and international news. After browsing the articles and editorials, I look for the most compelling piece on the wars in Iraq and Afghanistan. Rarely does a day go by without a healthy assessment of our progress (or lack of it), along with dissenting viewpoints about the safety of our troops and the viability of our so-called "exit strategy." When I find a well-written article that presents a logical dissent from our administration's position, I email it to President Bush and Vice President Cheney at president@whitehouse.gov and vice.president@whitehouse.gov, respectively.

Contrary to public opinion, I always receive a response; within a matter of minutes, the White House sends an auto-reply that thanks me for my letter. They also provide a link to the official White House website, where I can send additional comments to Dina Jenkins, the Secretary of Communications, and Harold Bodinger, my state representative. I use the links to send a suitable postscript to my original message, along with my suggestions to Rep. Bodinger for how to handle the "local angle" of the story. The entire process takes less than five minutes, but provides numerous benefits. First, President Bush gets two email messages from me every day, which provide intelligent, well-documented reasons for my opposition to the wars in Iraq and Afghanistan. Second, I also raise my concerns with my local representative, who can champion my views on the House floor. Third, by thoroughly analyzing the content on the CNN web site, I keep abreast of crucial national and international events, which makes me a better citizen.

My cynical friends are quick to tell me that my efforts are fruitless. Although they think that voicing a dissenting opinion is a complete waste of time, I don't buy it. My messages may not be scrutinized for details, but they are definitely counted and scanned for dissenting language. On a practical basis, they provide the initial spark of resistance, which, over time, will eventually evolve into a "buzz" or "grumbling" of significant magnitude. Every great debate in the history of our country started with the courage of a single person who was brave enough to express a dissenting opinion. I share their determination to engage in healthy, intelligent political discourse.

As a seventeen-year-old high school senior, I cannot stop the war, but I can certainly share my voice with anyone who will listen. Who better than the President?

Our Assessment: This author originally wrote this essay for a class assignment about political activism. With minor changes, it also worked well for his college applications. From the committee's perspective, the strength of this essay is the author's conviction. His actions, although far from unique, were focused, insightful, and intentional. His willingness to be an active and informed citizen was well perceived.

Political Activism   **(Common Application: 750 word limit)**

As an award-winning journalist, my father has written for the *Boston Herald* for thirty-eight years. Consequently, my siblings and I have always held a healthy respect for freedom of speech and expression. From my earliest memory, my parents taught us to view issues with a critical eye and to analyze news reports for their content, rather than sentiment. As a prospective journalism student, I have always taken those lessons quite seriously.

The events of September 11, 2001 tested my ability to view the news objectively. Although the media has always bombarded us with graphic images of suffering, this was different. My city was on fire and my friends and neighbors literally ran for their lives. In a split second, I lost every gram of desensitization that my father had instilled in me. Like many people in the United States, I was glued to my television set for weeks, watching commentators try to make sense of the devastating events. After seeing the bloody massacre re-played over and over again, I went to bed with a deep sense of foreboding about the future.

At the dinner table every evening, my father and I discussed what I had seen on television and why I was so sad and terrified. To my surprise, he did not share my fear and anxiety. When he ended our conversation one night, my father advised, "Read more than you watch." Rather than catch the morning news on television, he suggested that I read the *Boston Herald*. Unlike the visual reports, which were filled with emotional images and touching music, the paper offered a more objective source of information. It was my choice, he said, whether or not I lost sight of the truth in the story. If I continued to rely on the emotional "spin" of network news, I would give the gruesome pictures too much power. In his mind, the words told the *real* story.

My father was right. After that last sleep-deprived evening, I started to read local and national newspapers to put the events in their proper social and historical context. Rather than limit my perspective to that of mainstream journalists, I also scoured the literature for essays that were written by theologians, teachers and scientists. Whenever possible, I ignored the accompanying graphic images to ensure that I focused on the information, rather than the underlying emotion. Over time, my critical eye became more focused when I sat down to read. Eventually, I was able to put the terrorist attacks into perspective. America was down, but not beaten; with time, energy and healing, we would recover.

Within a few weeks, as my father predicted, I began to sleep better. I had re-claimed my power in a situation that left the rest of the world feeling powerless. Fortunately, as I read about opportunities for participation and service, I found a positive outlet for my creative energy. Rather than view myself as a victim, I began to see myself as a force for change. As the Adams High School chairperson of the 9/11 Relief Mission, I am part of a student organization that promotes peace through tolerance and education. We are eager to do our part to re-build our community in an environment of hope and peace.

Although I regained my sense of journalistic objectivity, I did not abandon the raw emotion that accompanied the devastating loss of 9/11. I am still deeply saddened by the images of suffering I see in nations across the globe and I am still brought to tears by footage of the collapse of the World Trade Center. I have learned, however, that the real story is not in the pictures, but the details. We only heal when we absorb the hope and truth of a situation, not when we wallow in emotion. Information is power, which makes it the strongest tool in a journalist's arsenal. Like my father, I am committed to using my power appropriately, by disseminating quality information with the highest standards of integrity and skill.

Our Assessment: This essay, although somewhat repetitive at the end, is unusually honest and thoughtful. From the committee's perspective, it was fascinating to read the advice that the candidate received from her father, who is an award-winning journalist. Ultimately, the candidate used that advice to resolve her issues with 9/11 and to confirm her own passion for journalism.

Political Activism   **(500 word limit)**

When my twin sister and I developed a web-based political show called Maryland Student Activist, we knew we would face formidable challenges to find a receptive audience. In the aftermath of 9/11, rumors abounded about the so-called "death" of the liberal media, including people's faith in the Internet. To many, it was foolish for us to even try to disagree with George W. Bush on any type of public forum. Thankfully, my sister and I were energized by this challenge. Although the odds were stacked us, we were determined to find a way to vocalize our fears and stand up for our beliefs. A low-cost web series, which would allow us to reach a global audience, was a terrific forum for two teenagers who wanted to participate in intelligent political debate.

Unbeknownst to us, my sister and I had separately found our way to Save the Feds, the aggressive antiwar campaign that was raising money and awareness on the Internet. My sister was intrigued by the effectiveness of their web site, while I admired the impressive caliber of people who had joined the organization. Clearly, Save the Feds knew the right way to bring intelligent people together to speak their conscience.

As we planned our debut episode of Maryland Student Activist, my sister and I each received a notice that Senator Barack Obama was going to speak to Save the Feds members at George Washington University. Surprisingly, we had never talked about being members of Save the Feds until that day. We attended the speech together and were heartened to see that dissent was not dead in America.

Inspired by Save the Feds' grassroots success and its astonishing use of the Internet, we doubled our efforts to launch www.MarylandStudentActivist.com. For most of 2006, we developed the program at a sound studio in Baltimore. Finally, in late October, we launched a preview website with an audio trailer. The response to the site was immediate and overwhelming; within a week, we received press coverage in the blogosphere and over 30,000 emails wishing us well from across the country. The next month, we launched an upgraded version of the site, complete with the first episode of our show, "Health Care Debacle: Can You Afford Coverage?" In our first six months, www.MarylandStudentActivist.com received more than 380,000 hits.

As we build our audience, we view the amazing saga of Save the Feds as a recipe that anyone can follow. Develop a clear message, then publicize it and manage it as it gains public awareness. Use every tool to spread the word, then harness the energy of enlightenment. After all, some of the most progressive ideas started out as one person's crazy dream.

Our Assessment: This author and her sister attracted significant media attention for their web series, which was heavily promoted during the 2008 Presidential elections. Consequently, it was not surprising that she decided to write a college application essay about her work on Maryland Student Activist. Ideally, the candidate *should* have used this as her primary essay, which had a longer length limit (750 words vs. 500 words). By using it as a secondary essay, she had to shorten it considerably. Nevertheless, she did an excellent job of explaining her accomplishment in less than 500 words.

Political Activism   **(500 word limit)**

As a child, my apathy regarding politics was a deliberate backlash against my mother, who was the most politically active person I knew. Every election year brought a flurry of activity in support of (or opposition to) a plethora of causes, from abortion and euthanasia to global warming and same-sex marriage. Regardless of the cause, my mother's position was inevitably impassioned and intractable; she devoted everything she had to support the candidate who shared her vision for the future. After sixteen years of her impassioned and idealistic speeches, I have reluctantly concluded that being an activist is not such a bad thing.

As I approach adulthood, I have developed a frightening perspective of the problems that my generation will face if the United States does not make some serious social, financial and political changes. As I watch the decisions that President Bush makes on our behalf, I am convinced that he must not be elected for a second term. To my mother's surprise, I also decided to put some muscle behind my idealism; I offered to accompany her to a rally for Senator John Kerry in the Bangor area. I had read several articles about Kerry that convinced me that his combination of values and leadership experience made him the best candidate to beat Bush. Although it was the last weekend before finals, I was willing to take a break from studying in order to support his campaign.

Upon our arrival, we discovered that John Kerry wasn't the only Democratic candidate scheduled to appear; the convention hall was already filled with zealous supporters for Dick Gephardt, Howard Dean and Retired General Wesley Clark. Sometimes, our offers of Kerry literature were met with abrupt responses: "No thanks, I'm for Howard Dean." A few people grudgingly accepted our flyers, but I silently questioned whether or not we were accomplishing anything. An impromptu conversation changed everything.

When I overheard the man next to me discussing the pros and cons of John Kerry, I offered him more information. He initially refused, but a few minutes later, he decided to read my flyer that contained Bill Clinton's endorsement of Kerry. Soon, the man and I were excitedly discussing "our guy's" proposed plan for national health insurance. An hour later, John Kerry gave an impassioned speech that literally brought the crowd to its feet. I was completely energized by the hopeful and humorous political discussions that I had enjoyed. By the end of the evening, my mother and I sprinted to the parking lot, proudly wearing our John Kerry buttons.

How amazing I felt that night! After handing out nearly 500 flyers and chatting with dozens of kindred spirits, I knew that I had made a difference. Even more compelling, I was ready to make a financial contribution to Kerry's campaign. Before the rally, I had planned to spend my $200 in savings on a trip to New York City with my friends; it seemed foolish to "waste" it on a political donation. Afterward, however, I recognized that my contribution really *could* make a difference. After seeing the commitment and excitement at the rally, I was proud to sacrifice my hard-earned money to support my candidate of choice. Although I won't be able to vote for two years, politics directly affects my life, my school and my community. I am honored to make a difference.

Our Assessment: Many candidates write about their interest in politics and their first experience at a rally. This young lady did it as well as we've ever seen. Her intelligence and enthusiasm made a huge impact on the admissions committee.

Political Activism (400 word limit)

In June of 2008, I listened to a speech by Democratic presidential candidate Barack Obama, in which he challenged Democrats to stand up to the Republican Party's reckless international and economic policies. Afterwards, I called his campaign headquarters to see how I could support his efforts. The woman who took my call said there was no official office in Utah, but she suggested that I join a local group of Obama supporters.

Shortly afterwards, I received an email from Joe Dorsey, the chairperson of Obama's fledgling support group in Provo. At first, I hedged about attending the gathering; I had never been involved in politics and didn't know anyone who planned to attend. The evening of the event, my father shooed me out the door with a dismissive, "Just go."

The other four attendees were as diverse as they were intelligent: a nursing instructor, a software engineer, a rabbi and a college professor. Although we had very different backgrounds, we were all determined to take the country back from the moneyed interests that had hijacked the Republican administration.

Our first objective was to hold a party fund-raiser during the following month. My job, in addition to sending out notices, was to clarify the local and federal restrictions about raising money. I called the national headquarters of the Obama campaign, who explained the rules about money they could (and could not) accept. The phone call left me wildly energized. Although I was just a high school student, I was going to make a difference. I was going to do my part to help the Democrats take our country back!

For the first time in my life, I was optimistic about politics. I realized that the "system" could only work if more people got involved. Accordingly, I was determined to encourage other disenchanted citizens to participate. Our next meeting had thirty people; the next, eighty-five; the next, nearly three hundred. As I suspected, there were more people like me who were eager to initiate change.

Since then, I have done everything possible to champion Obama's candidacy; I have signed petitions, volunteered at polling places, and promoted him door-to-door. In my tiny conservative town, I was proud to be one of Obama's youngest and most vigilant supporters. With every act on his campaign's behalf, I felt like I was doing what I was created to do.

Our Assessment: This essay is short, focused, honest, and optimistic. It also explains the candidate's interest in a political career, which his recommendation letters highlighted. The committee was particularly impressed by the author's willingness to extend himself to join the Obama campaign, which did not have an office near his house. Rather than make excuses, he took the initiative to find a group that could put his talents and passion to good use.

A Change You Will Make in Your Community   (400 word limit)

Due to the reckless actions of a drunk driver, my best friend Stephanie was paralyzed from the neck down at age fifteen. While riding home from a movie, she was hit head-on by a minivan whose driver's blood alcohol was twice the legal limit. Because her injuries were so severe, Stephanie was forced to withdraw from Barrington High School and enlist the help of a full-time tutor. There is little chance that she will ever enjoy her previous hobbies of dancing, field hockey and swimming.

Stephanie's injuries left a lasting impression on my heart and those of everyone in our tight-knit community. Although we are a small town, we have survived a disproportionate number of drunk driving fatalities. We all vowed that Stephanie's devastating accident would be the last. Following her accident last year, 20 of us formed the town's first chapter of Students Against Drunk Driving (SADD). Sadly, our first step was making peace with the fact that the person who hit Stephanie was not an evil monster; he was actually a 20-year-old native of our community who we had known our entire lives. Before the accident, we also knew that Joe liked to drink on Friday nights at the County Line Saloon. Ironically, we never took the time to consider whether Joe had a problem that could potentially hurt others. As a result, we didn't stop him from getting in his car and driving home after 3, 4, or 10 mixed drinks.

SADD does everything possible to spread awareness about the potential ramifications of drunk driving. Unfortunately, we can't undo the traumatic incident that led to our group's formation. Despite our heartfelt intentions, Stephanie will never walk again and Joe will spend the next eight years in prison, where he will receive no help or treatment for his alcoholism. The net result? Two wasted lives from a needless and preventable situation. SADD's goal is to prevent the next incident - to prevent more wasted lives and ruined families.

I am committed to being Stephanie's friend for the rest of my life. I visit her frequently and try my best to be a normal presence in her very narrow world. Yet I am equally committed to working for SADD, to prevent other kids my age from making the same mistake as Joe. Barrington has zero tolerance for drinking and driving, which can have devastating consequences. For the rest of my life, I will do my part to protect my family and friends from this reckless decision that affects every level of society.

Our Assessment: The strength of this essay is in the details. The author had a vested interest in joining SADD due to her best friend's injuries. Amazingly, she was also compassionate enough to see the situation from the drunk driver's point of view. Her demonstrated commitment to SADD made a positive impression on the committee.

A Change You Will Make in Your Community   (500 word limit)

Like most teens, I am immersed in a culture that romanticizes drugs and alcohol. In high school, many of my friends have encouraged me to experiment with drugs, but I have never wavered in my decision to say no. In the fifth grade, I heard a riveting presentation by a local D.A.R.E officer, who described the effects of drugs on the human body. I couldn't imagine that anyone could listen to his moving speech and still want to do drugs. Later, in Driver's Education class, we watched videos that showed the deadly combination of drinking and driving. The graphic images reinforced my decision to remain abstinent.

The issue became personal to me during my freshman year in high school, when my cousin was critically injured in a drunk driving accident. Only three of the five passengers in the car survived, including the driver. Although he lived, my cousin was hospitalized for months with a serious head injury and broken leg. In an instant, his life was permanently changed. My cousin still struggles with short-term memory loss; he also has a plate in his leg to hold his shattered bone together. When I visited him in the hospital, I was afraid of what I saw – it looked like there was an erector set protruding from his kneecap. I was pained by the horrible damage that a night of drinking had caused.

Ironically, I also felt compassion for the terrible consequences that the drunk driver has faced. For the rest of his life, he will carry the weight of two violent deaths and my cousin's injuries on his shoulders. The driver was also held criminally liable for the accident, which will diminish his future professional and financial opportunities. He will be haunted forever by the effects of one bad decision. After watching the ramifications for both my cousin and the guilty driver, it has become easier for me to say no to drugs and alcohol.

My commitment to abstinence shapes my social life in a positive way, because I surround myself with other people who have similar values. Needless to say, it isn't always a popular choice. Public service announcements claim that people will respect you for saying no to drugs and alcohol, but that isn't always true. From my experience, people can be offended if you turn it down and will exclude you from their group.

In the past few years, my commitment to abstinence has cost me friendships, party invitations and acceptance into certain cliques – but it doesn't matter. I respect myself and am proud of my decision. I won't let other people influence my better judgment. In my generation, the choice to drink and do drugs is a challenge that every teen must face. I am eager to promote the benefits of an abstinent lifestyle and reap the benefits of that decision.

Our Assessment: At first blush, this essay may seem very similar to the previous one, because both writers discuss the impact of a drunk driving accident on someone close to them. But this essay caught the committee's eye because of the penultimate paragraph, in which the author admitted that "saying no" was not a popular decision in her social circle. By admitting that, the candidate revealed a rare level of honesty – and an admirable strength of character. It set this essay apart from several others on the same topic.

A Change You Will Make in Your Community   (400 word limit)

Lakeland Skating is a free program that my high school class created for underprivileged youths in Los Angeles. We provide after-school and summer activity for kids age 6 - 15, and support talented younger players who cannot afford to pay for skating lessons. I was one of the five founding members of the program, which was inspired by a similar initiative in my native Chicago. To raise awareness and money for Lakeland Skating, we solicited donations from dozens of businesses throughout Los Angeles. We also overcame several obstacles to bring Lakeland Skating to fruition.

At first, our potential volunteers and benefactors were reluctant to support a program that did not have any sort of track record. They also questioned our ability (as teenagers) to manage such an ambitious venture. During meetings, I ultimately used my youth to my advantage. I gained their interest by demonstrating an organized and structured plan as well as an infectious enthusiasm for the project. To finance my first set of classes, I used creative ways to raise money. I organized a charity skating tournament at Lakeland School, where I charged entrance fees and awarded cash prizes. I also convinced Lakeland-area businesses to pay for sponsorships. As awareness grew, our donors contributed money, additional schools and community centers referred their children, and we attracted numerous volunteer teachers. Within two years, the program expanded from a 5-member team to a 25-employee enterprise that operates across five Los Angeles sites and touches the lives of more than 150 children.

This experience was personally rewarding because it gave me the opportunity to give back to the community in a tangible way. Before we formed Lakeland Skating, many of the children had limited opportunities to create success in their lives. My program provides a positive outlet for them to learn valuable lessons in teamwork, compromise and hard work. I am convinced that the benefits of launching a community initiative are self-perpetuating: the more we help underprivileged kids, the greater the chance they can succeed and subsequently use the tools we provide them to improve their own lives and their communities. Lakeland

Skating is the perfect way for me to use my talents as a skating instructor to make a positive difference in society.

<u>Our Assessment</u>: This author also used this essay to answer questions about a personal achievement, her greatest passion, and her most rewarding outside activity. By highlighting her initiative and leadership skills, the author presented herself as someone who was unusually focused, mature, and goal-oriented.

A Change You Will Make in Your Community   **(400 word limit)**

As a first-generation Chinese-American, I am committed to helping new arrivals adjust to life in the United States. For the past two years, I have accompanied my mother to the Chinese-American Support Center, which is a mecca in San Diego for new arrivals from mainland China. Although everyone has the proper visas and documents to legally live here, few understand English well enough to function independently in American culture. My goal is to help them survive the adjustment and thrive in their new homeland.

At the Center, I play with the children, teach them songs, and conduct basic lessons in English. I also read to senior citizens, who are eager to stay abreast of news from their homeland. Since Chinese newspapers are unavailable here, I translate articles from the *Los Angeles Times* and the *San Francisco Chronicle* about relevant social and political topics. I also conduct an informal class in American culture for high school students and young adults.

For teenagers, "fitting in" requires an understanding of the trends in American clothing, slang, music and other types of entertainment. My role is that of a supportive friend who shows new arrivals the social opportunities that abound in San Diego. I take groups of Chinese teens to rock concerts, football games and the beach. I also explain the relevance of SAT exams, Ivy League schools and community colleges. In tough times, I remind new arrivals that America is a land of unlimited hope and opportunity. Regardless of their age, sex, financial status, or religious beliefs, the only thing stopping them is their willingness to pursue America's endless opportunities.

Although my language skills are not perfect, I feel a sense of accomplishment by helping others. After years of volunteering at the Chinese-American Support Center, I have learned that giving a warm smile to a scared child can provide trust and comfort. I have also reconfirmed my appreciation for my parents, who made the bold choice to leave the comfort of China and raise me in the United States. I am committed to sharing my love and friendship with other people who have taken a similar risk. With the help of the Chinese-American Support Center, I will "pay forward" the kindness and generosity that was so lovingly given to me.

<u>Our Assessment</u>: This is a lovely essay that showcases the author's kindness, generosity, and willingness to help others. In the penultimate paragraph, she also shows her understanding of the social aspects of assimilation, which are particularly difficult for many teens to master. Her work at the Center is a tangible benefit to the Chinese-American community.

A Change You Will Make in Your Community   **(500 word limit)**

I live in a community that buses its students to a regional high school that is more than twenty miles away. Due to the recent tax shortfall, our Town Commission eliminated the bus service for those who lived within five miles of the campus. Suddenly, without transportation to a school that is four miles away, I became a vocal enthusiast against the arbitrary five-mile limit.

I vocalized my displeasure during an after-school "informational" meeting at our Town Hall. Sadly, although dozens of parents attended, no one was courageous enough to speak up…. except me. I cited the hazards that the decision created for 400 kids, who were forced to walk a long distance on a busy road with no sidewalk. On rainy and snowy days, we are vulnerable to passing cars, whose drivers can barely see us. Finally, there are health and hygienic issues that the commissioners had never considered. Every day, we arrived at school feeling and looking like drowned rats after our four-mile obstacle course/endurance walk. I appreciated the community's need to save money, but not at the expense of my own safety.

I would love to say that I was so persuasive at that meeting that the Town Commissioners immediately restored the bus service. Unfortunately, it was not that easy….. yet I refused abandon my goal. Instead, I became the unofficial spokesperson for the situation when I gave an interview to our local newspaper and to a reporter from the local television station. When the Associated Press picked up the story, I was invited to appear on two nationally syndicated news shows. Soon, our town was famous for more than its excellent dairy products; we were the short-sighted community that failed to transport their "fine children" to school. Not surprisingly, our bus service was restored just two weeks after my national television debut.

I learned several lessons from this experience. First, shame works. The commissioners already knew the drawbacks of the plan and the danger to the children before they eliminated the bus service, but they did it anyway. The financial "bottom line" was a higher priority than our safety. Even worse, the commissioners only decided to honor our needs when they were shamed into doing so. Knowing this, I am convinced that it is every citizen's responsibility to direct the actions of our elected officials. We must be ready, willing, and able to defend and assert our rights.

Finally, I learned that I am an articulate spokesperson for change. Unlike the worried parents at the meeting who were too afraid to speak up, I am willing to assume the spotlight and use my voice for those who are afraid or unable to speak. Ironically, before I lost my bus ride, I wasn't inclined to "rock the boat" to initiate change. Thanks to this experience, I discovered a hidden strength and a strong resolve, which will greatly enhance my personal and professional future.

Our Assessment: This author took the initiative to champion a change that benefited numerous students in his community. His final two paragraphs, which explain the lessons that he learned by doing so, were particularly effective. For another application, the candidate used this same essay to answer a question about his leadership experience.

A Current Event or Issue   (500 word limit)

For my research project in my AP Civics class, I investigated the impact of the "achievement gap," which costs the U.S. between $350 and $425 billion dollars in GDP each year. The largest contributors to this gap are minority children, who currently comprise nearly 45% of our school-age population. As a first-generation college student who was raised in an Arabic-speaking household, I understand the challenges these students face to succeed in a foreign educational system. Without positive mentorship and support, the achievement gap can be nearly impossible to bridge.

When I researched this dilemma, I was determined to find a viable way to narrow the gap in my own community. In 2009, I launched a non-profit organization called A World Without Limits (AWWL), which provides academic mentorship to the students who need it the most. On a theoretical basis, the goal of AWWL is to give all children, regardless of their race or socioeconomic status, an equal opportunity to succeed in the classroom. On a practical basis, I also hoped to provide poor and minority children with academic resources that are beyond the reach of their inner city schools.

Through one-on-one coaching and mentoring, AWWL empowers students to realize their intellectual capacity and pursue their college aspirations. Historically, inner-city students from low-income communities have under-performed on most standardized exams, which limits their access to the most prestigious college preparatory programs. In many communities, this type of academic segregation begins as early as middle school. AWWL aims to level the playing field by providing inner-city students with an academically-focused culture that offers them adequate time to master the skills they will need to qualify for top programs. We also provide positive mentorship and role-modeling to help students appreciate the opportunities that they will enjoy if they continue to excel in school.

By design, A World Without Limits promotes the virtues of perseverance, higher education and intellectual curiosity in all of its participants. When they join the program, each student is matched with a college-level volunteer who has enjoyed a successful academic career. Through meetings and tutoring sessions, the mentors share their insight and advice about the educational process. By doing so, they provide the students with a critical support structure that is rarely available in inner-city schools, which lack the financial resources for outside programs and role-modeling. AWWL fills this void by emulating the strengths of non-profit organizations such as Teach for America and REACH, which maximize our ability to provide meaningful academic opportunity in poor communities.

After a successful two years, I am excited about the many ways that AWWL can expand its reach and make a lasting impact on the communities we serve. With the support of my faculty and peers, I believe that it has the capacity to provide meaningful, cost-effective educational intervention in hundreds (and perhaps thousands) of inner-city classrooms. Eventually, organizations such as AWWL can narrow the achievement gap and change the lives of millions of youths in the United States, who have the ability and desire to transform their dreams into reality. I am thrilled to do my part to help guide the way.

<u>Our Assessment</u>: This candidate used the same essay to answer questions about his goals and leadership experience. From an admissions perspective, it worked well for all three prompts. The candidate identified a problem and took the initiative to try to solve it in his own community. This is exactly the type of creativity and independent thinking that top schools are looking for.

A Current Event or Issue   (600 word limit)

The continuous economic growth in Bahrain, which has been fueled primarily by the oil and real estate industries, has made a great improvement in the nation's standard of living. However, the nation's health care system remains substandard and unreliable. Despite a population of nearly three million people, Bahrain only has a handful of small hospitals. Few of them receive funding from the federal government, which limits the technological advancements they can offer their patients. There is also a dire lack of training, licensing, and regulations for the health care professionals who are responsible for treating and diagnosing a wide range of illnesses and injuries. As a result, thousands of patients die in Bahrain every day because of improper medical care.

An additional complication is the misplaced priorities in health care. In Bahrain, the system is governed by money, rather than ethics. Regardless of the severity of the case, patients who have money are always treated first. Those who do not have money are unlikely to be treated at all. In April of 2011, my two cousins got into an auto accident while visiting our extended family in Bahrain. Yan's foot was severely crushed, which required immediate medical treatment. Lee rushed her to the nearest hospital, where she hoped that Yan would receive proper care and compassion. Sadly, the doctors refused to treat Yan until the hospital received $3,000 USD. To obtain this amount of money, Lee had to leave Yan alone at the hospital for several hours while she waited for treatment. If she had not returned with the required fee, Yan would likely have died in the waiting room.

Ironically, wealthy and insured patients also struggle to obtain quality care. Last winter, my grandfather was hospitalized in Bahrain with severe abdominal pain. The facility that admitted him had the highest standards of care in the nation. During the first week, my grandfather's doctors prescribed medication for irritable bowel syndrome, which they insisted was the source of his pain. Unfortunately, his condition continued to deteriorate. Nevertheless, the doctors sent my grandfather home with a stronger medication and told him to "have faith" in their diagnostic skills. The cost for his hospital stay, in which his condition only got worse, was $30,000 USD. A week later, when he returned to the U.S., my grandfather sought treatment for the same symptoms at a public hospital in New York City. Within a day, the doctors determined that he had a carcinoid tumor in his colon, which was the source of his discomfort. My grandfather's condition improved greatly after its removal. Sadly, his case, which is far from unique, reveals the poor training and unethical practices of health care professionals in Bahrain.

Because of the high cost and unreliable reputations of many doctors, the people in Bahrain often buy their medication directly from the pharmacy, where all drugs are available without a prescription. Sadly, the pharmaceutical industry is not well regulated in Bahrain, which makes this approach inherently risky. Although the law requires that all pharmacies have a government license, many owners obtain them by bribing local officials or falsifying their application documents. Then, these unqualified owners engage in deceptive practices to increase their profits, such as diluting the medication and changing the expiration date in order to sell old medication. There is also a knowledge gap, which prevents the average citizen from choosing the correct drug and dosage for their particular illness. As a result, people often exacerbate their problem by choosing the wrong drug, taking it incorrectly, and ignoring potentially deadly side effects and drug interactions.

Although the public is well aware of these issues, the federal government continues to ignore them. If they invested money in the health care system and enforced strict regulations on the standards for care, medication, and the training of health care professionals, considerable pain, suffering, and loss could easily be prevented.

<u>Our Assessment</u>: This is a serious, well written, and well documented paper about an important issue in the author's native country. Because she was applying to a highly competitive public health program, it was also a highly relevant (and somewhat unusual) topic for the admissions committee. By adding the personal

anecdotes about her cousins and grandfather, the candidate gave this essay the detail it needed to be persuasive and memorable.

A Current Event or Issue   (Common Application: 750 word limit)

When I first arrived in the United States, I was impressed by the opulence of Los Angeles International Airport, which was a starting contrast to the ramshackle one in Vietnam. Clearly, in this utopian society, the rumors I had heard were true; people had truly escaped the shadow of poverty that permeates the rest of the developing world. However, after living in America for several years, I have realized that many Californians also struggle to pay their bills and find affordable housing. Despite its superficial wealth, this seemingly perfect nation has its fair share of poverty and homelessness.

As I became accustomed to life in Los Angeles, I realized that the homeless are treated with more dignity in the US than Vietnam, where there is no "safety net" for people who have fallen upon tough times. Across LA, there are many shelters, soup kitchens, and relief organizations to fulfill the needs of disadvantaged people. In my junior year, I worked at a Salvation Army soup kitchen in order to give back. Every day, I noted the grateful smiles on the faces of the people we served. At first, I believed that these acts of goodwill were a solution to their problems. However, when the Salvation Army closed the soup kitchen due to a budget shortfall, our customers were back on the street with no one to feed and shelter them. This extreme poverty, which had a profound impact on me, caused me to investigate the underlying causes of homelessness in my AP Civics class.

The problem, it seems, is the way that our social and economic models deal with people who lack the resources they need to stand on their own two feet. Without an education, these individuals cannot obtain the well-paying jobs they need to afford a secure place to live. To solve their dilemma, they need a way to become financially independent, rather than rely on others for their basic needs.

When I searched for potential solutions, I discovered the principle of microcredit, which is used by bankers in developing nations to stimulate economic growth. By nature, banks are unwilling to loan money to people who have little cash or income. As a result, those who wished to start their own businesses cannot do so without a significant amount of collateral. With microcredit, however, special banks and organizations extend small loans to aspiring entrepreneurs. The money can be used to pay for the start-up costs of the enterprise, which will enable the owner to become self-sufficient. To reduce the risk of default, the government guarantees the individual's payments for the loan over a specified period of time and provides free training in all aspects of small business management.

To me, this is a risk-free way for the banks to help disadvantaged people literally transform their lives. In rural India and Pakistan, local bankers have lessened the effects of poverty by introducing this revolutionary financial product in the nation's poorest regions. Recently, several non-profit organizations in San Francisco have used a similar approach to ensure their own sustainability. I am convinced that microcredit would also work on a national level in the United States and Vietnam, where many people struggle to survive. By researching this concept, I realized that the catalyst is simply goodwill. If a bank is willing to implement a microcredit program, which earns a lower rate of return than other investments, it can improve the quality of life for local residents. Anyone can have this impact on society, if he is willing to become part of the solution.

In my own community, I have made a difference by working in a soup kitchen and raising funds for my church, which performs mission work in my native Vietnam. In college, I hope to acquire the knowledge and skills I will need to create financial products such as microloans that can empower individuals to become self-sufficient. By working closely with the businesses and charities that serve the homeless, I hope to find better ways to bring essential resources to the people who need them the most – one person and one solution at a time.

Our Assessment: This middle of this essay is somewhat technical, but the beginning and ending include the author's own thoughts and experiences, which provide enough of a personal touch to engage the reader. The essay also shows that the author has considerable insight into the economic realities of both nations and the need for creative change (such as microcredit). By choosing this topic, which was directly related to her interest in economics, the candidate differentiated herself from other applicants who were applying to the same program.

A Current Event or Issue   (600 word limit)

Like many students, I was terribly shaken by the terrorist attacks of 9/11, which came at a time when I felt particularly lost and vulnerable. Several of my friends sought refuge in drugs and alcohol, which provided a temporary respite from their grief and pain. Others became consumed with thoughts of revenge, either through a direct attack on Osama bin Laden, or through the eventual war in Iraq. I, on the other hand, simply felt paralyzed by the senseless destruction of everything that I held dear. I couldn't imagine how I could possibly survive with the terrible pain in my heart.

In my darkest moment, I knelt on the floor of my room and considered the question of my faith. In my first sixteen years of life, I had not given much thought to my religion or what I believed. However, a long talk with my pastor had produced storms within me that needed meaningful answers. All at once, I knew that I wanted to live a life that would honor God. The clarity of that moment made me weep. Rising from my knees and wiping the tears off my face, I realized that I had changed in only a few moments. My decision to become a Christian was a momentous turning point in my life, which had a permanent impact on my outlook.

Embracing God and the Christian faith ignited an intellectual fire in me that brought with it an unquenchable thirst for knowledge. I voraciously read every theology book I could find; I was particularly inspired by Saint Augustine, who saw "all truth as God's truth." With this in mind, I decided to become a teacher who would guide and nurture young minds from a Christian world view. By expanding my perspective of world issues, I would be better prepared to engage the minds of my future students and answer tough questions about the actions of those who defy Gods' laws.

Emotionally, my discovery of God has given me a more compassionate attitude towards others. The Bible teaches us that all individuals are created in the image of God and are thereby worthy of dignity and respect. From this lesson, I developed a feeling of responsibility for those who suffer and need help from others. With this in mind, I began to visit senior citizens at one of the retirement communities in my city. Each Saturday, I spend time talking to them and helping them perform their daily functions. I have also started to volunteer at my church, where I serve as a youth leader and an assistant to the pastor. As a leader, I feel a deep sense of satisfaction as I see the children develop good moral character.

Ever since that first moment of understanding, my faith in God has served as my driving force to reach my goals. It has armed me with a clear vision of who I want to be and what I want to do with my life. Because of this inner determination, I have managed to earn top grades while working a part-time job and devoting time to my church and community. My beliefs have taught me to view every challenge as an opportunity to grow as an individual and to inspire my family and friends with the strengths that my faith gives me. How we live reveals the deepest convictions about the world. Since 9/11, I have offered my life as proof of my convictions. As for the terrorists, I am leaving their fate in God's hands, who will eventually deliver the ultimate judgment.

<u>Our Assessment</u>: We are often asked if candidates should write essays about their religious and spiritual beliefs. Depending on the author's intention, it may (or may not) be risky. Our best advice is to remember the goal of the essay, which is to reveal your best self to the reader. If your essay is positive in nature, helps to explain your character, and promotes a spirit of love and inclusion, then it will not offend anyone. But if the essay is opinionated or divisive, it may not be worth the risk. This essay works because it is sincere, concise, and informative. It helps the reader understand who the author is and what she will bring to the school that accepts her.

A Current Event or Issue   (500 word limit)

As she turned to leave the room, eight-year-old Erica raised her arms for one last hug. "I love you, Sara. Thank you for listening." My heart burst with happiness as I watched my young playmate jump into her mother's car to go home. As a volunteer for Kids United, where I work with troubled children, I was honored to play a role in making Erica's world "right" again.

As the child of two physicians, I was raised with a powerful desire to serve others. Unlike my parents, however, my passion is not medicine, but the legal and sociological aspects of family life. Like many children of divorce, I grew up with many unanswerable questions about what it means to be a family. Despite my parents' earnest explanations, at age 6, I was simply too young to understand why my father no longer lived with us. My lifelong efforts to cultivate positive relationships within a fractured family have not only made me a stronger person, but inspired me to help others who are struggling with similar situations.

As a high school freshman, I accompanied my mother on a humanitarian trip to Guatemala, where she provided medical care to poor and underserved communities. After helping her in the clinic each day, I was delighted to provide an empathetic ear to the local children. In this impoverished environment, in which food and medicine were unattainable luxuries, my own problems seemed selfish and immature. I was privileged to become part of the children's lives, if only for a short period of time. As I listened to their stories of real human suffering, I was compelled to make a difference. By the time I came home, I had acknowledged my calling to provide emotional support and encouragement to children in disadvantaged situations. Throughout high school, I have volunteered at Kids United, where I counsel children who have academic and social problems. By working closely with third graders like Erica, who need the benefits of personalized counseling, I help them to develop good study habits and to handle their problems at home. I have also confirmed my interest in becoming a child psychologist, so that I can make a meaningful difference in my clients' lives.

As a child, I did not understand the concept of "sole custody" in a divorce decree; now, I am aware of the ramifications of this decision on the daily lives of every family member. Many children are defeated by their parents' divorce, because their needs are not addressed. As a psychologist, I can help to ensure a better future for children whose lives have been disrupted by divorce and abuse. I want to provide a voice for those who did not cause the discord, but are most directly affected by its implications.

Our Assessment: The author used this essay for several prompts, including questions about her long-term goal, favorite outside activity, and personal (and familial) influences. It was well perceived.

A Current Event or Issue   (500 word limit)

On September 13, 2001, I struggled with a miserable combination of shock and numbness after the attack on the World Trade Center. My pain for the victims was exacerbated by the sad realization that the United States was going to seek revenge for the terrorist attacks. Regardless of how or where we responded, thousands of innocent people, who had nothing to do with the attack, would lose their lives. To me, the ramifications of this type of retribution were unthinkable.

I desperately wanted to stop the cycle of violence. At first, I considered writing to President Bush to urge him to use restraint in response to the attacks. Upon further thought, I realized that my letter would never make it through the bureaucracy at the White House. Still, I sat down at my computer and began to type the letter. In a moment of inspiration, the words flowed easily. An hour or so later, I mailed the letter to the White House, and as an afterthought, I also emailed it to a few friends.

The response to my email was overwhelming; to my surprise, my friends and family members forwarded it to almost two hundred people around the world. Within a week, I began getting positive letters and emails from kindred souls in Europe, Africa and Asia. Clearly, my message of peace had struck a chord. I was astonished and gratified by the thoughtful responses to my letter.

A college student from China named Ling Li asked me if I would be willing to publish my letter as an ad in a major US newspaper. I agreed. Within a day of receiving my approval, she organized a group of like-minded people called the Student Peace Initiative to solicit donations to have my letter published in *USA Today*. When I learned that full-page ads can cost more than $200,000, I doubted that we would succeed, but Ling Li was determined to meet the challenge.

The Student Peace Initiative gained momentum with help from organizers in Japan, China, Great Britain, Germany, Brazil and the United States. Soon, we published a website and began to communicate with Global Veterans for Peace, which was also counseling caution in our foreign policy. To my delight, my letter was published as a full-page ad in the October 12, 2001, edition of *USA Today*.

The public response was immediate and overwhelming. First, the principal of my school asked me to discuss my letter in front of the School Board. Then, I received interview requests from several radio stations, newspapers and television stations, which gave me more attention than I ever dreamed possible. Since then, Ling Li and her associates have moved forward with the Student Peace Initiative, and I am now an honorary member of Global Veterans for Peace. We continue to work for a peaceful world in which all people enjoy a safe and secure future.

Our Assessment: This essay shows that a small gesture can have a big impact on the global community. It also touched the committee's hearts in a memorable way. By attaching a copy of his original email message (and the subsequent newspaper ad) to his application, this author reminded his readers of their own feelings of helplessness after the 9/11 attacks. They were impressed to know that he was the one who had expressed a desire for peace and compassion during such an uncertain and traumatic time.

Chapter 4: A Person, Fictional Character, or Creative Work that has Influenced You (and Why)

One of the essay questions for the Common Application asks candidates to discuss a person, fictional character, or creative work that has influenced them (and why). Additionally, several top-tier colleges also ask this as a secondary question on their own applications, with a relatively rigid length limit (250 words or less). Finally, an alternative question at many schools asks students to discuss a famous quotation or piece of advice that has special meaning to them. Like many prompts, these questions are open-ended. Depending upon the side of yourself that you want to show the committee, you can write about almost anyone. What, then, makes a good answer to this question?

First, you should pick an individual, character, or creative work that exemplifies your deepest personal values. If you pride yourself on your sensitivity and compassion – and you cultivated those qualities by emulating a friend or relative, then that person may be a good topic for this essay. Likewise, if an historical figure or character in a movie or novel has inspired you to be more generous, ambitious, and socially aware, then they are another possible topic. Ideally, you should choose someone who is a positive example, rather than a negative one. (Occasionally, we see effective essays that take the opposite approach – the authors tell a cautionary tale about someone who has made significant mistakes in life - but this is risky. If you take this approach, be sure to pick someone who eventually turns his/her life around and displays positive qualities, such as strength, insight, and resiliency.)

Second, do not ignore the second half of the question, which is to explain why (and how) this person, quotation, or creative work has influenced you. As always, the power is in the details. If you say the person is witty and clever, you must give concrete examples that show his/her humor and intelligence. If possible, try to relate the anecdotes to your own life and the problems that you face. If written honestly and openly, these essays can reveal a lot about who you are, what you value, and who you eventually hope to be.

The following essays vary widely in length and topic, but they all handled this question in an extraordinary way. By design, we have grouped the essays in the following sub-categories:

Personal Role Model
Discuss a Meaningful or Inspirational Quotation
Discuss Your Favorite Book or Character

For each essay, we have also indicated whether or not the essay was written for the Common Application or to answer a specific question on the application for an individual college or university. (Note: If the essay was for a specific school, we have also indicated the specified length limit for the response.)

To protect the privacy of the writer, the names of all people, classes, schools, places, teams, activities, and companies have been changed.

Role Model / Influential Person   (400 word limit)

Several years ago, I became intrigued by my grandmother's stories about her childhood in the Shawnee Indian tribe. The most vibrant tales were about Angelica, my paternal great-grandmother, who died before I was born. According to my grandmother, Angelica had progressive ideas that were uncommon in her day and age, such as a woman's right to pursue a career and obtain an education. Long before these issues were considered fashionable - or even acceptable, she lobbied tirelessly on their behalf.

When I asked to see a picture of my great-grandmother, I was saddened to learn that few had ever been taken. Yet my grandmother was delighted to paint a vivid picture of her mother on the canvas of my mind. On a physical basis, she claimed that Angelica looked just like the woman on the Indian head nickel; she had prominent cheek bones, a bold nose and a strong jaw that gave her face character. Like many women of her day, Angelica was just over five feet tall, with shining black hair that nearly reached the floor.

Even more impressive was Angelica's role in preserving the tribe's history. During the late 1800's, when most of the 20+ Indian tribes in Nebraska were transferred to reservations in Kansas and Oklahoma, several Shawnee tribes stayed in southern Nebraska. Around this time, Angelica began to work as an agent of the Bureau of Indian Affairs in Dodge City. Although few agents at the time were actually Indian, my great-grandmother possessed the requisite language skills to do the job. Angelica distributed health supplies and helped to establish schools, but her real talent was helping people become useful citizens. At a time when few women had careers, my great-grandmother encouraged them to build better lives. Angelica also helped the remaining Indian population integrate into the mainstream American lifestyle by serving as the bridge between two highly disparate cultures.

After hearing so many stories about my great-grandmother, I smile whenever I see "her" image on an Indian head nickel. What a wonderful role model Angelica must have been for the other women in her tribe! As a child of the twenty-first century, I have never had to fight for educational and professional equality. Likewise, I have never faced physical, emotional, and socioeconomic segregation because I am Native American. Nevertheless, I am honored to know that one of my ancestors was a true pioneer who devoted her life to the service of others. As I embark on my own career in education, I will be guided by Angelica's heartfelt belief that with hard work and determination, all things are possible.

Our Assessment: This is a lovely and sensitive essay about an ancestor that the author had never met, but felt that she actually "knew." Thanks to the many details she provided, the reader understands why the candidate's great-grandmother was an inspirational role model.

Role Model / Influential Person   (1,000 word limit)

When I was fifteen, I got my first job selling ice cream at the Dairy Queen down the road. It was one of those seasonal places that opened for the hot summer months, then closed for the winter while the owners retreated to Florida. When I accepted the job, I saw it as a golden opportunity to earn the cash I would need to cover the expenses of my entire junior year.

My colleague at the ice cream counter was Mrs. Walker, a spry 80-year-old who had more energy than people a quarter her age. By the time I met her, Walker had survived the Depression, two World Wars, and four subsequent decades without aging in any observable way. Although she had a touch of gray hair, Mrs. Walker also possessed a level of stamina and good health that made life worth living at eighty. She is truly someone who gives "old people" a good name.

I didn't know any of this the day I met her, of course. I just saw an old lady who somehow didn't have the sense to stay home and watch soap operas. What in the world did she think she was doing hustling ice cream at the Dairy Queen? And how big a dent would she put into my plans to pick up as many girls as possible?

Not surprisingly, I wasn't particularly receptive when Mrs. Walker started to talk about her life. Instead, I grunted polite responses to her stories about outliving two husbands and raising six kids during the Great Depression. What a downer, I thought, as I chased the thought of economic deprivation from my mind. As part of a middle-class family, I couldn't relate to the concept of people starving in the US. How could anyone starve when ice cream was just 50 cents a cup?

During my second summer at the shop, Mrs. Walker seemed less spry than before, and I wondered if old age was finally catching up with her. I politely asked if she was OK, praying silently that she wouldn't burden me with some horrible tale of cancer or heart disease. She assured me that she was fine, but had a few things on her mind. I didn't pursue it. Instead, I listened patiently to her lectures about the importance of delivering superior service that made people smile. Although I nodded politely, I thought it was the corniest thing I had ever heard.

Mrs. Walker left early that summer, unexpectedly for me, but not to our regular customers who knew her well. She volunteered for a missionary program in Colombia, to care for children that had been orphaned by the recent earthquakes. When I heard the news, I was humbled to learn that Mrs. Walker's three sons were missionaries there, who had been presumed dead after the first quake. For three agonizing weeks, she waited patiently for confirmation of their status without saying a word to me. In my heart, I wondered what "other things" I hadn't bothered to ask her about.

Fortunately, Mrs. Walker's sons survived, but overwhelmed her with tales about the sick and orphaned children who needed help from emergency personnel. Few volunteers were eager to accept an assignment in a country such as Colombia, which was plagued by health and political problems. According to my parents, it would truly take a saint to do it. Mrs. Walker didn't hesitate to accept the challenge. I'm not sure what impressed me the most: maybe that she had raised three sons who were altruistic enough to become missionaries and devote their lives to helping others. Possibly that at her advanced age, Mrs. Walker still felt a calling to do something meaningful (even heroic) with her life. I was amazed that she would risk life and limb to save children she didn't even know. Further, I was humbled to know that Mrs. Walker had silently weathered the potential loss of her sons without expressing her fears to anyone else. And, amazingly, throughout this trauma, she still found the time and energy to try to teach me some compassion.

Before I met Mrs. Walker, I had never taken the time to get to know anyone outside my own privileged world. My idea of starvation was being served dinner an hour late; a tragedy was not having enough money to buy a new CD. I felt ashamed of myself when I saw what a valuable contribution she was making to the world, long after most people had hung up their hats and retired to the golf course. I knew in my heart that I had missed a golden opportunity to learn from her during our two summers at Dairy Queen, when I focused on meeting girls.

I won't make that mistake again. In two weeks, I am organizing Mrs. Walker's welcome home party when she finally returns from Colombia. Afterwards, I am eager to learn more about this special woman who takes impossible risks on behalf of the people who need her the most. After missing out on so many opportunities to get to know her, I hope that she will be gracious enough to give me a second chance.

My minister once said that people get their guidance from God at the most unlikely times and places. He also said that angels walk the earth among us, but we are rarely able to recognize them. In my wildest dreams, I never thought that I would meet an angel in my job at Dairy Queen. But I did, and her name is Mrs. Walker.

<u>Our Assessment</u>: This essay, although extremely long, gives the reader considerable insight into the candidate's growth and development. By explaining the impact that Mrs. Walker's story had on his own life, this author gave us a window into his heart that we would never have learned about any other way. The writing style, which was extremely simple, made the essay easy to read, which was also appreciated by the admissions committee.

Role Model / Influential Person   (500 word limit)

Throughout my life, I have been blessed with many exemplary role models, including my devoted parents, a strong extended family, and several generous teachers, coaches and ministers in my community. During our discussions, I have acquired the benefit of the collective wisdom they have acquired through decades of life experience. As a result, it is rare that I find someone my own age that inspires me to emulate them, but Cassie Bernard is that rare exception. Her exemplary behavior during a terrifying attack made her an extraordinary person and role model.

After the Columbine High School shooting, people across the globe grieved the loss of 17-year-old Cassie and a dozen of her classmates, who were brutally murdered by two of their peers. Those with strong Christian beliefs have cited Cassie as a martyr, because she confirmed her faith in God to her killer right before he shot her. I am touched by this knowledge, and know in my heart that Cassie's faith has been an inspiration to her family and friends.

I look up to Cassie not only for her faith, but for the courageous way that she lived. At the time of her death, Cassie was reportedly on the right track. She was a good student, a devoted friend, and an unwavering Christian. But life hadn't always been easy for her. During puberty, Cassie fell prey to the temptations of drugs, sex and alcohol. For nearly a year, she fought with her family, abandoned her faith, and dabbled in the occult.

Thankfully, at age sixteen, Cassie acknowledged her poor choices and asked her parents and minister to help her find her way back to God. This could not have been an easy step for her, yet Cassie overcame her addictions and surrounded herself with people who would love her and nurture her life rather than destroy it. Her courage, strength of character, and remarkable resiliency made her subsequent death at seventeen even more heartbreaking.

I can relate to Cassie on several levels. Although my school is academically strong, it is not immune to the problems created by drugs, alcohol, and peer pressure. Cassie's story helps me to resist temptation and stay on the right path. I am particularly inspired by her ability to acknowledge her mistakes and seek help. I also respect her decision to end destructive friendships and establish new ones. Most importantly, I am impressed by Cassie's successful return to the very school where she had previously had so much trouble. I don't know if I would have had her confidence in a similar situation.

When I think of Cassie, I try not to focus on her tragic death, but on her successful life. She was honest, brave, loving and talented. As a teenager, she survived mistakes and problems that most adults could not overcome. I am certain that as Cassie matured, she would have become a strong woman and a leader in her community. As a Christian, she would have devoted her life to serving God and helping other teens stay on the right path. Cassie showed great courage in death, but even more courage in living a life that wasn't nearly as easy or uncomplicated as it looked on the surface. For that reason alone, she was an extraordinary role model.

Our Assessment: After the Columbine shootings, many candidates wrote about the impact of the event in their admissions essays. This candidate did an excellent job of explaining how one of the victims, who she didn't actually "know," was a positive role model for her. The examples and reasoning, which the author relates back to her own life, are particularly strong. Few essays on the topic revealed a comparable level of thought and sensitivity.

Role Model / Influential Person   (500 word limit)

Athletes, rock stars, politicians. The highest-paid anchorwoman on CNN. For many students, the most influential people in their lives are the "role models" that have been carefully created by the media. They are the actors who win Academy Awards, the Senators who fight for a cause and the musicians who give concerts for charity. Ignoring this all-pervasive media blitz, I have actually been more influenced by a distant relative who lived on another continent for most of my life. Looking back, a seemingly insignificant encounter with my maternal grandfather played a pivotal role in shaping the woman I have become.

As a young child, I did not have daily contact with my relatives like most of my friends did. With the exception of my uncle, all of my extended family lives in Sweden, which makes it harder for us to stay in touch. Every few years, we visit them and try to catch up on each other's lives. When I was twelve, we took my grandparents to a seaside resort called Arcadia. After visiting the aquarium, my grandfather decided to wait in the car while the rest of us took a walk on the beach. When I returned, I found him looking at the wall that divided the sand and the parking lot. He asked me to sit next to him because he wanted to show me something.

As I sat, my grandfather explained that the wall was full of shells that had been pushed into the cement. He described how fossils were made and why it was important that we have them. As I sat there talking with my grandfather, the time flew by. We didn't even notice that the rest of the family had taken a detour to the local ice cream shop. After we returned to the hotel, my grandfather continued to tell me about the rare fossils he had found during a dig near the coast of Turkey.

Our conversation did not have special significance to me until my grandfather's death four years later. When I thought about the day we spent together, I realized that our talk at the resort was one of the few private conversations we ever had. A distinguished archeologist, he often gave dry monologues about fossils that were snooze-fests to the rest of my non-scientific family. I was the only one who had showed the slightest interest in the field that he loved.

In hindsight, the significance of our talk was not about fossils; it was a rare chance to spend time with my grandfather and absorb just a small fraction of his knowledge. Archeology was his passion, which he was excited to share with me. I wish I had been mature enough to ask him questions about a topic that he obviously loved. Our brief talk made me realize the importance of every conversation and the meaning behind small gestures.

Looking back, my grandfather's love of science was the catalyst to my own professional aspirations. His excitement about fossils inspired me to study them for my senior project; I am now applying to college with an eye on a research career. Through this experience, I learned that a role model can appear in our lives when we least expect. Just because the person is not rich and powerful does not mean that they can't influence our lives.

Our Assessment: This essay is simple, honest, and touching. It also gives the reader some insight into why the candidate was interested in scientific research. The candidate used the same essay to answer questions about her favorite childhood memory.

Role Model / Influential Person   (Common Application: 750 word limit)

I met my most cherished role model when I fell off a pair of parallel bars and landed with a sickening thud on the protective floor mats beneath us. If I think about it for too long, I can easily remember the shooting pain down my right arm as I tried to brace my fall. I would like to say that I recovered immediately and jumped back up on the bars, but that wouldn't be true. But Seth did, and he did it with a smile.

Seth and I are not athletes and I can safely say that we never will be. We met at the University of Miami rehab facility for patients with spinal cord injuries. Seth and I had both suffered nerve damage from separate car accidents within a few days of each other. Although we had never met before, we became roommates at the facility and friends for life.

Seth's damage was far more serious than mine; consequently, he knew from day one that he faced an uphill struggle. Although several of Seth's vertebrae were intact, he faced extensive physical therapy to regain partial use of his legs. In a heartbeat, his days as an avid tennis player and teenage heartthrob were over, at least for awhile. Even worse, Seth's heartbroken parents worried endlessly about how they would pay the costs of his extended care. But to meet Seth, you would never dream that he had such a dire prognosis. His playful disposition belied the long and painful road ahead of him.

My reaction to my injury was very different. Before the crash, I was a 16-year-old daredevil who had lost control of my car during a blinding snowstorm. My parents had pleaded with me not to drive that night, but I insisted that I could handle the car for the three miles between our house and work. It's amazing how wrong I was. Fortunately, an orthopedic surgeon repaired the bones in my leg without any complications. In the following months, the rigid physical therapy schedule gave me a new meaning for the word "pain."

At first, I didn't know why I was so incredibly angry. I wasn't going to die or lose my leg, but I was filled with rage because this was happening to me. Before the accident, I had always prided myself on being a responsible and successful person. When I put my mind to something, I could do it better, faster and more creatively than anyone else. Now, I couldn't stand, walk, or go to the bathroom by myself. I couldn't even keep a 1999 Suzuki Swift on the road in a snowstorm.

For more than a week, I wallowed in self pity. I turned the corner the day that I met Seth. Here was someone a lot like me: young, smart, funny and talented, who was going through the exact same thing. As kindred spirits, we bonded the only way we could: by competing. My life focus became doing better than Seth. If he could do nine leg lifts, I had to do ten. If he survived ten minutes of massage, I had to have fifteen. We coordinated our therapy sessions for the same days and times and found that it really improved our mood.

Thankfully, the doctors supported anything that helped our progress. On the toughest days, Seth was always an inspiration for me. When I succeeded, he cheered, and when I wanted to give up, he challenged me to keep going. Sadly, as I began to make serious progress, I didn't realize that he had hit a plateau. After three months, I was able to leave the rehab center and return home. At the time, I did not realize that Seth would never leave his wheelchair. We talked by phone every day, but he never let on that his prognosis had been downgraded. After awhile, Seth's family moved him to a group home a few hours away, where he could switch his focus from recovery to adjustment. By the time I made plans to visit Seth, he had already moved.

Seth is my role model for many reasons. He survived a debilitating accident without showing anger or self-pity. Instead, he retained his sense of humor and devoted his energy to helping a stranger get well. At a time when most people, including me, would be "takers," Seth offered unlimited friendship and support. Most impressively, he accepted an unenviable fate with incomparable grace and dignity. To me, Seth was the ultimate survivor.

It isn't often that I meet another person my own age with so much character and maturity. I am proud to call Seth a friend and I wish that I could do more to help him. Two years later, we continue to call, write, and text each other nearly every day. His legacy to me is his selflessness. Whenever life knocks me off the parallel bars, I will think of Seth and pick myself off the mat and keep on trying. After coming so far, he would expect nothing less of me.

Our Assessment: This is a detailed and heartfelt discussion of a friendship born of shared pain. By telling Seth's story in such an upbeat manner, the candidate gave us a window into his soul. He also confirmed his own ability to survive a terrible setback.

Favorite Book, Character or Historical Figure   **(300 word limit)**

At age seven, I struggled to learn a new language and overcome racial discrimination in my new country. Since then, I have always enjoyed "fish out of water" stories about children who have faced similar obstacles. My favorite is the novel *Dragonwings* by Laurence Yep, which captured my early sense of sadness and isolation. *Dragonwings* tells the story of Moon Shadow, an eight-year-old Chinese boy who comes to America to live with his father. Delighted to move to the "land of gold," Moon Shadow is stunned by the subsequent realities of racism and language barriers in 1906 Chinatown. Speaking only Mandarin, he endures terrible teasing as he tries to adapt to American culture. Yet Moon Shadow secretly shares his father's determination to control his destiny and ride the wind.

After moving from Guatemala to Texas, I suffered the same painful isolation as Moon Shadow. My classmates mocked my efforts to learn English, which caused a persistent case of shyness. I eventually overcame my self-consciousness by joining my school's nationally recognized choral group. As I perfected my vocal talent, I performed in several concerts and gave voice lessons to other aspiring singers. By reaching out to others who needed help, I realized that my feelings of isolation were far from unique.

Dragonwings eloquently describes how Moon Shadow followed a similar journey to adapt to his new culture and help others become more tolerant of diversity. As the novel closes, he overcomes formidable obstacles to achieve his dreams. A decade later, the story remains a powerful allegory for my own life. By learning a new language and becoming a seasoned vocalist, I also gained control of my destiny. Like Moon Shadow, I became free to ride the wind.

<u>Our Assessment</u>: This essay eloquently compares the problems that Moon Shadow faced to those in the candidate's own life. By doing so, it offered a moving answer to the question.

Favorite Book, Character or Historical Figure   **(250 word limit)**

The last book that thoroughly inspired me was Neale Walsh's *Conversations with God*. Although it took me three nights to finish it, the book was well worth the lost sleep. For the first time in my life, I felt that a writer was speaking to me directly: not just to my mind, but to some unspoken voice deep within my soul that was determined to reawaken. What a wonderful and joyous feeling!

Walsh's book captured my interest because he offered a different interpretation of God's message from the one presented in the Bible, Torah, and other religious writings. As a lapsed Catholic, I have been searching for spiritual direction for many years, but I have not found any meaningful answers in religious texts. Walsh's book answers many of the "big" questions that I have about God, his expectations of us, and life after death. After reading his message of hope, I truly felt God's love for me for the first time in my life.

The book is written in a simple, conversational style that makes its message easy to accept and understand. Most importantly, it speaks to all people, regardless of their particular faith, and offers a message of hope and unity. I wish that more people would embrace its message of an all-inclusive God. Since the beginning of time, humans have fought countless wars due to their religious differences. Each side believes that "their" god is the only one with a sure path to salvation. *Conversations with God* reveals the futility of these divisions, which ignore a profound universal truth - God loves us all, regardless of our religious affiliation.

<u>Our Assessment</u>: Without this essay, the committee would never have known about the candidate's quest for spiritual guidance and direction. Her mature insight about the book gave them an heightened appreciation of the diversity she would bring to the campus.

Favorite Book, Character or Historical Figure   **(300 word limit)**

The fictitious character I would most like to emulate is Atticus Finch from *To Kill a Mockingbird*. Despite his intelligence and education, he eschewed the wealth of the big city to devote his life to helping the residents of a small town. I can't help but consider him to be a powerful role model. Although he is a supporting character in the novel, Mr. Finch best demonstrates the power of goodness, honesty and wisdom. I put the book down wishing that I knew more about him.

I imagine that at age 18, Mr. Finch was a lot like me. He lived in a small town, where he planned to return after college and make a lasting contribution. He was probably quiet in high school - hard-working, yet appreciative of the simple pleasures that a rural life would offer. An avid fisherman, Mr. Finch loved to tease the neighborhood girls while he baited their hooks with "yucky" worms. Like me, he probably had a special place in his heart for one of those girls, yet he was not confident or outgoing enough to ask her out. Instead, he rationalized the consequences of his shyness. There would be plenty of time for dating and romance when he completed his education and had time to consider his own needs. As a shy young man with a comparable personality, I believe that if I had known Mr. Finch, we would have become good friends.

As I apply to college and consider my future, I am eager to mature from a young and awkward teenager into an accomplished and confident professional like Mr. Finch. In college, I will enjoy unlimited opportunities to expand my confidence and sophistication. Along the way, I plan to use Mr. Finch as a personal role model. In all situations, I will try to be a loving friend, a generous citizen and a productive man; when faced with a moral or ethical dilemma, I will follow my conscience rather than succumb to my own short-term pleasures. Hopefully, by doing so, I will grow into a man as honorable and inspirational as Atticus Finch.

Our Assessment: This essay stands out because the author actually compares himself to the character and notes their many personal similarities. By taking this approach, the candidate gives the reader a closer look at his own goals and values.

Favorite Book, Character or Historical Figure   (Common Application: 750 word limit)

Through a filter of depression and self-imposed isolation, *Catcher in the Rye's* Holden Caufield provides a wry and cynical perspective of coming-of-age in America. Nearly fifty years after its initial publication, the book continues to capture the universal sense of fear and rejection that we all must overcome to achieve our respective dreams. Although my personality is nothing like Holden's, I was inspired by his refusal to blindly surrender his individuality. He taught me the importance of expanding my world and setting aggressive goals, regardless of anyone else's opinion.

Many of Holden's psychological problems stemmed from his inability to accept and resolve conflict. Fortunately, I was blessed with an abundance of resources, both financial and emotional, to build a successful life. From an early age, I knew that I would encounter many obstacles on my path to success. Rather than wallow in idealism like Holden, I use my talent and creativity to overcome the barriers in my way. Armed with a strong personality and a sense of determination, I never let anyone restrict my goals or dreams.

One of my earliest goals was to become a championship runner. At age twelve, I was scheduled to compete in two events, and I needed to place in the top six to be eligible for the championship. When the results of my first race were announced, I discovered that I missed qualifying by just a fraction of a second. Aware of my disappointment, my teammate tried to comfort me. "Maybe you're just not fast enough this year." I was determined to prove her wrong. Several minutes later, as I prepared for my second event, my heart pounded, my stomach churned, and my mind raced out of control. As I awaited the start of the race, I had a single thought. "Prove her wrong." When the results were announced, I discovered that I had exceeded my own expectations. I won the event. I learned an important lesson that day about being empowered by failure. Blessed with a strong will, I never give up.

Six years later, I continue to race competitively on my school's track team, which has won first place in the state competition for the past three years. Last summer, I also began to coach top runners at a private girl's school, who have amazing athletic talent. When I am working with a student who questions her ability or confidence, I reinforce my powerful childhood lesson about perseverance. *"Defeat never comes to any man until he admits it."* Buoyed by a strong will to succeed, my students inevitably become confident runners with a passion to win.

One poignant aspect of Holden's personality is his idealistic vision of himself as a protector of innocent souls. In the book's most famous quotation, he fantasizes about saving their pure spirit. *"I'm standing on the edge of some crazy cliff..... I have to catch everybody if they start to go over.........I'd just be the catcher in the rye.......".* While I don't consider myself a savior, I share Holden's dedication to helping those around me. Since the fifth grade, I have been a dedicated volunteer in my community: as a YMCA tutor, a hospital worker, in a soup kitchen, and through my church's youth council. For the past two years, I have also volunteered at a local hospital, where I handle administrative tasks and provide direct patient care. Every person I meet offers an opportunity for me to share my strengths and to learn something new.

As I prepare for college, I am grateful for the many blessings in my life, including a loving family and a supportive school environment, where I am an individual, rather than just a number. With their nurturance, I have survived the adolescent pain and isolation in which Holden Caufield became entrenched. In future endeavors, I hope to embody the best of Holden, including his commitment to authenticity and his desire to help others. With the support of my family and church, I am eager to embrace the spirit of altruism in the Harvard community. In addition to pursuing professional success, I am committed to being a woman of integrity and honor. I will become the sincere, self-actualized person that Holden Caulfield could only imagine.

Our Assessment: Few candidates answer this question on the Common Application, because they do not know how to include themselves in a discussion about a book or character. This exceptional essay shows how it is done. By relating Holden's traits to her own values and goals, this candidate shows the reader an impressive level of maturity and insight. She also had the confidence to tackle an unusual essay question, which gained the reader's interest and respect.

Favorite Book, Character or Historical Figure   (300 word limit)

I cried the first time I read the novel *Black Like Me* and continue to be moved by it today. Growing up in rural Wisconsin, I was isolated from most racial issues and never realized how polarized our culture was. *Black Like Me* made those issues impossible to ignore.

I was raised to believe that God loves all people equally, regardless of our superficial differences. Consequently, I would like to think that my treatment of another person would not change because of the color of his skin. *Black Like Me* forced me to question whether that was true. Although the protagonist's clothing, intelligence, material wealth, and behavior were consistent in the book, the treatment he received from others was not. When he appeared white, he was accepted as a valued citizen, while he was subjected to horrible abuse and cruelty when he appeared black.

Besides making me sad, this forced me to look at the way I evaluate others when I first meet them. I was disheartened to realize how much my perception was affected by external factors that were beyond the person's control – and certainly not indicative or his (or her) character. If I had not read the book, I might not have recognized my own tendency to equate the trappings of wealth with intrinsic strengths that cannot be bought at any price.

Black Like Me forced me to take an honest look at the darkest parts of my heart, which I rarely have the inclination to do. After recognizing my own weaknesses and prejudices, I am determined to promote equality in our society for all people in their pursuit of success. I can't change the world, but I can certainly change my own attitude and behavior. Thanks to this book, I know that acceptance, unity and change can only be achieved one person at a time, one interaction at a time. I am committed to doing my part to create a more cohesive and equitable society because of *Black Like Me*.

Our Assessment: This essay, although somewhat idealistic, explains the book's effect on the candidate's thoughts about race. From an admissions perspective, it provides information that would be impossible to get any other way.

A quotation, phrase, or statement that has influenced you.   (500 word limit)

In her haunting ballad, "Sailing through the Sorrow," Marissa Dodd escaped the tedium of daily life by "going to a land of paradise." After hearing the song for the first time, I pondered the many different places that people visit for comfort and reflection. Thoreau had Walden Pond, Caesar had his Forum and Buddha had his Bo tree. And I, Raymond Velez, have the Valdosta Creek.

To escape the heat of Georgia's summer days, I often sought refuge in the mysteries of the nearby creek. Nearly fifty feet from our narrow backyard, it was hard to see from the road, and as far as I could tell, I was its only visitor. From my perch on the water's edge, I sat beneath two large pine trees, which provided refuge from the blistering sun. As I watched the ripples and currents, I noticed how the stones and pebbles on the shallow bottom allowed the water to glide in creative patterns over their smooth surfaces. Larger, moss covered rocks dotted the bank and provided ideal spots for an inquisitive child to watch and wonder.

By the creek, my mind was free to ponder any topic. One day, while I silently watched the birds, I pretended that I was one. As my body lay still, my imagination took flight; looking down on the creek from the pale blue heavens, the wind whistled over my face and the sun warmed my body. I also wondered how the birds decided to land at this particular creek. Was it the availability of food? The solitude? I wondered if they noticed me and if I was part of their attraction. By the time my eyes flickered open, it was time to go home and finish my chores. I left my questions about the birds at the edge of the creek, which was the only possible place to find the answers.

The creek was also a frontier, because it extended deeper into the woods than I had ever explored. As a child, I thought that if I wandered into its darkness, I might be consumed by it and never be heard from again. As I gradually overcame this fear, I embarked on numerous expeditions using my father's old compass to guide my way. By the time I was twelve, I had followed the Valdosta Creek for six miles, nearly all the way to Meigs. Clearly, as my body grew in height and weight, my boundaries had also expanded.

By my senior year of high school, the creek that was once a wondrous expedition for me was simply a narrow barrier between my house and a sprawling new development. As our community grew, one of the costs of "progress" was the tiny wooded area that had served as a "land of paradise" throughout my early summer days. Fortunately, by the time I was forced to leave the creek behind, I had found other quiet places to meditate and explore. Yet the Valdosta Creek will always be special; I will cherish its tranquil lessons, whatever stream, river, or ocean I ultimately choose to wade.

Our Assessment: In this essay, the candidate used the original song as a springboard to his discussion of his own "land of paradise." The writing, although somewhat flowery, was also quite creative. The essay was well received.

A quotation, phrase, or statement that has influenced you.   (500 word limit)

Few will have the greatness to bend history itself; but each of us can work to change a small portion of events, and in the total of all those acts will be written the history of this generation. - Robert F. Kennedy

On the first day of school, I cringed when I discovered that I had been assigned to Dr. Wyatt's section of American History. I had already heard about him from my older sister and her friends; the man was a heartless tyrant who assigned way too much homework and who rarely gave out A grades in his A.P. courses. Although I was eager to learn, I felt sucker-punched by the idea of trying to meet his unrealistic expectations.

In hindsight, being assigned to Dr. Wyatt's course was the defining point in my high school career. Granted, he made me work hard, but he also taught me how to think independently and to put world events into their proper perspective. From the outset, he took an aggressive stance in discussing twentieth-century politics. To keep us from gravitating towards empty categories like liberal or conservative, he encouraged us to thoroughly discuss each issue before we took a stand on it. Imagine my surprise when I, the daughter of two conservative parents, discovered that I had strong liberal tendencies! I cherished the opportunity to discuss relevant topics with someone whose goal was not to convert me to his position, but to help me clarify my own. Thanks to Dr. Wyatt, I have become a more informed citizen with a passion for responsible social reform.

Dr. Wyatt also taught us how to make sense out of history by evaluating the personal motives behind a given chain of historical events. In his class, I came to the realization that history isn't just a series of names and dates in a textbook, but a complex subject that requires deep thought and analysis for full comprehension. Upon further discussion, I was forced to acknowledge that some of the "best" U.S. Presidents made the "right" choices at the wrong times, which came to be viewed as failures. Other times, by taking the "safe" road, our leaders saved themselves from humiliation, but left the country vulnerable to preventable risks. Only in hindsight can we say with any degree of certainty that any given event (or President) was good or bad, and even then, the perception may not be unanimous. What some Americans view as a victory, others see as a heartless betrayal.

Dr. Wyatt's greatest lesson to me was demonstrating my own role in the evolution of American history and politics. As a U.S. citizen, I have a responsibility to be aware of the issues affecting our country and to do my part to champion them. Although one person cannot single-handedly change the world, (s)he can certainly raise awareness and promote discussion about the needs in his/her community. Every major change in

American culture began with the grassroots efforts of a single person who thought that the world could be a better place. It is my job, as an educated American, to create the change that I believe is necessary. Thank you, Dr. Wyatt, for letting me know it is possible.

<u>Our Assessment</u>: With minor changes, the candidate used the same essay to answer questions about her favorite class and an inspirational role model. As always, the power is in the details. By explaining the types of discussions that Dr. Wyatt encouraged, which allowed the candidate to cultivate her own beliefs, the author recognized her responsibility to change what is wrong (rather than simply complain about it). It is a powerful message.

A quotation, phrase, or statement that has influenced you.   (600 word limit)

I have never known any distress that an hour's reading did not relieve. - Montesquieu

My first beloved books were the Disney Encyclopedia volumes. At age four, I wasn't old enough to read them, but I always wanted to have them read to me. In fact, I memorized the ten-volume set, so that when my parents tried to skip a page, I would jump in and recite the missing passages. After learning to read on my own, my favorite book became the anatomy volume in the Sesame Street Library. Courtesy of a mail-order offer, I was the only first grader who knew what a placenta was. As I grew older, I continued to read voraciously, because it taught me so much more than what I learned in school.

Since grade school, my extensive reading has also sparked my interest in science. Every day, I walked to the library after school and browsed a different book. By the fourth grade, I had read all of the chemistry books that contained fewer than 300 pages; by the sixth grade, I had mastered Einstein's Theory of Relativity. During that time period, I became so interested in biology that I sold cookies door-to-door to raise enough money to buy my own microscope.

As early as the third grade, reading also helped me in school. When offered a chance to receive extra credit for outside reading assignments, I was determined to earn more stars than anyone else in the class. The rules were fairly straightforward; every sixty pages counted for one star of credit, and fifteen stars would yield an "A" grade. With my love of books, I quickly seized my chance to shine. Rather than read many short books, I devoured 300-page sagas by Laura Ingalls Wilder. When everyone else got 18 stars, the little tag with my name on it had over 50 stars. This inner drive and competition still motivates my work today, but unfortunately, my teachers no longer award stars for effort or performance.

Amazingly, my most satisfying reading has been outside of school, when I technically don't "have" to read. If left to my own devices, I will devour at least one or two pleasure books per weekend, from genres as diverse as French cooking to true crime novels. Through this exploration, I have discovered that books are powerful teachers. Nonfiction titles have quenched my curiosity about political issues and have exposed me to a host of new ideas and information. Novels, on the other hand, have given me a deeper understanding about the past, including the struggles of new immigrants and the humanitarian goals of 19th century labor unions. In the pages of books, I have visited battlefields in Europe, witnessed female "rites of passage" in northern Africa, and observed the atrocities in Nazi concentration camps.

Ironically, my family often worries about my reading selections; if given the chance, they would limit my choices to "happy" books that inspire "feel good" moments and improve my self-esteem. But, to me, that is like moving to a city to avoid the "bad" parts of town. Despite our desire for perfection, troubled situations exist, even if they don't directly touch our neighborhoods or our lives. Books can introduce us to these problems and help us to understand another reality, both the beautiful and the ugly. Most importantly, they can inspire passionate debate and responsible action. What better way could I spend my spare time?

<u>Our Assessment</u>: Although the beginning is somewhat tepid, this essay has a strong ending and provides considerable detail about the candidate's personality.

A quotation, phrase, or statement that has influenced you. (400 word limit)

"No matter what you do, you must always be the best." As the child of two immigrants who came to the US with nothing but the clothes on their backs, I was constantly reminded of the many opportunities available to me in America. To earn them, I simply needed to work harder, faster, and more diligently than I ever dreamed possible.

Although my parents lacked an education, they demonstrated this value to me through their commitment to their jobs, family, and community. By being the best parents, neighbors, workers, and citizens, they set an impressive example for me to follow. Yet, surprisingly, the evidence of this mindset was not always visible. On the outside, we were identical to many other Cuban-American families in our neighborhood in Bensonhurst. The only difference was our willingness to think big. Thanks to my parents, we enjoyed a level of optimism and success that belied our modest appearance.

For my parents, "being the best" meant leaving the security of their native land to pursue a tenuous future in America. Without knowing a word of English, they came to Brooklyn in 1988 and began their steady progression from blue-collar factory workers to successful owners of their own dry cleaning business. By pursuing their dream, they learned how to overcome obstacles relating to language, money, and racial discrimination. By handling these problems with tact and skill, they taught me to be proud of what I do and to never assume that my work is trivial. Even mindless tasks, such as sorting hangers and emptying trash cans, must be done reliably and correctly for a business to succeed.

As a student and athlete, this inner drive continues to motivate my actions. It forced me to try hard in school although I didn't know a word of English. It also encouraged me to stick with the soccer team even though I was one of the smallest boys on the field. By giving my best and sticking through the hard times, I developed my skills as a student, athlete, and campus leader. There is no doubt in my mind that I will succeed in my chosen profession as well.

Thanks to my father's mantra, I have the optimism to survive whatever difficulties that life may hand me. I also have the wisdom to see opportunity where others see hard work. Most importantly, I know that "being the best" sometimes means hanging in there and keeping the faith until the dark clouds have finally passed. By doing so, I can make a difference.

Our Assessment: If you are going to quote a family member, you must be willing to explain the significance of the quote in your own life. This author did an extraordinary job of explaining how his parents gave every activity the best they had to offer, regardless of the obstacles in their way. Over time, he internalized their inspirational mantra as his own. It is a simple story (and message), but a very powerful one.

Chapter 5: A Personal Experience that Illustrates the Diversity you will Bring to the Campus

Many colleges ask candidates to explain the factors that have shaped their identity – or how they will contribute to the diversity on campus. Other schools ask candidates to explain their fit for a particular major or program; out of all the options you have for your college education, why did you pick them? If you encounter this question (or some variation of it), you must provide an answer that is focused, detailed, and persuasive, regardless of the length limit. Ideally, the information you present should complement – rather than duplicate – the material in your other essays for that school.

As always, the power is in the details. For the diversity question, you should tell your life story in a creative and entertaining way. Bear in mind, diversity encompasses far more than just race; it also refers to your interests, talents, upbringing, religion, hobbies, family size, hometown, travel experiences, and socioeconomic standing. No two candidates have had the same life experiences, which is what makes this question interesting. If written honestly and openly, this essay can reveal a lot about who you are, what you value, and who you eventually hope to be.

The following essays vary widely in length and topic, but they all handled this question in an extraordinary way. By design, we have grouped the essays in the following sub-categories:

Factors that Shaped Your Identity
An International Travel Experience
How You Will Contribute To Campus Diversity
Your Fit for a Particular School

In each case, we have also indicated whether or not the essay was written for the Common Application or to answer a specific question for an individual college or university. (Note: If the essay was for a specific school, we have also indicated the specified length limit for the response.)

To protect the privacy of the writer, the names of all people, classes, schools, places, teams, activities, and companies have been changed.

Factors that Shaped Your Identity   (600 word limit)

In the small town of Lancaster, Alaska, which is 200 miles north of Anchorage, we have few of the resources of the "lower 49." That's where ingenuity comes in. My forefathers were an industrious bunch who savored their independence, yet acknowledged the need to augment the town's resources. In 1977, a small group of locals, including my newly married parents, solicited funds from our county seat to finance the first local library. Then, they negotiated a lease for a 400-square-foot trailer on the northeast corner of our town square. Since June 1978, 223 Main Street has been our local library – and my favorite place in the world.

Due to limited funding, the library only has one paid employee. The rest of the work is handled by volunteers like me, who card books, organize shelves and serve a steady stream of patrons. In my three years at the library, my greatest achievement has been reading nearly every book that we have. The benefits have been enormous. Through the power of literature, I have had the opportunity to visit places that are far away from rural Lancaster. I began with the Nancy Drew mystery series, which revealed the amazing way that a teenage girl could reason her way out of any situation. By age ten, I had progressed to the Alice Dwyer series that chronicles a family's journey across Europe during the World Wars. Dwyer's stories, which moved me beyond belief, brought my history lessons to life in a magical way. While my classes required me to memorize names, dates, and battles, the Dwyer books revealed the devastating effects of each event on the *people* in each region. They also gave me a new respect for the soldiers who were brave enough to fight in the wars.

Since my freshman year in high school, I have been thoroughly enraptured by Shakespeare. Although I found his style intimidating at first, I have come to love his eloquent prose. I also marvel at the classic nature of his work. How many authors have produced characters and stories that we remember centuries later? And who else but Shakespeare could redefine our language and introduce so many new words, phrases and cliches? Without his work, my life would have a terrible void that would be impossible to fill.

Sadly, our library faces daunting challenges to survive in a world of diminishing state and local funding. This past year, I assumed a leadership role in our fundraising efforts by soliciting donations from townspeople and conducting used book drives in three surrounding towns. I also developed an inter-library loan program, which has given us access to thousands of new titles. After a lifetime of reading enjoyment, I am eager to preserve that benefit for younger Lancaster residents.

As I apply to Harvard, I am excited by the many social, educational, and financial resources that the campus offers its students. But nothing excites me as much as the Harvard libraries, which will give me access to more than one million books in hundreds of academic disciplines. From my childhood in Lancaster, I know that the written word is powerful enough to transform human lives. It has certainly broadened mine. In addition to its myriad educational benefits, it has also given me the confidence to leave Lancaster, knowing that I am as educated and well-versed in cultural and world events as someone in Paris, London, or Sydney. As long as I can read, I can travel anywhere, learn anything, and enjoy the wisdom of brilliant authors throughout history. Whenever I have spare time, you can find me at the Lancaster Community Library.

Our Assessment: This essay conveys significant information about the candidate's life in a rural town and the importance of her local library. After reading it, the committee knew that she would make exceptional use of the library system at whatever university she chose.

Factors that Shaped Your Identity   **(500 word limit)**

I first picked up a violin at age six and haven't put it down since. Well, maybe to bathe and to sleep, but otherwise, I'm committed to playing it for the rest of my life. Surprisingly, I am not a child prodigy or even from a musical family. I began playing the violin because I saw it on television and begged my mother to let me try it. She acquiesced, thinking that it was an impulse or a short-lived lark. Twelve years later, we're still screeching along.

My first lesson did not suggest that I was a professional musician in the making. I found the violin difficult to handle and even harder to play. But I knew from my first lesson that this was the instrument for me. With my teacher's help, I began a romance with musical instrument that would eventually change my life. My parents always supported my passion, no matter how loud and screechy my practice sessions.

Sometimes I get stuck on a piece and can only master it by playing the same six or seven chords repeatedly. My brother handles these phases with industrial quality ear plugs, while my parents have become immune. At my loudest moments, they console themselves with the knowledge that it's at least classical music. "Better than that awful heavy metal stuff" my dad will say. I don't have the heart to tell him that the Stones tour with a full orchestra.

As a musician, I particularly enjoy learning a new piece and performing it for a receptive audience. I currently perform with two groups on a regular basis: my high school band and the Broward County Junior Symphony. The symphony, in particular, challenges me as a musician and provides invaluable opportunities for me to play with others who share my passion for music. For the past six years, I have played a difficult twenty-number set for their statewide Christmas concert series, which includes a selection of traditional carols and international holiday pieces. I have a short solo in three numbers that is particularly nerve-racking. For nearly sixty seconds, I must focus only on my bow's careful dance with the string, which produces a haunting resonance that I can feel deep in my soul. For a split second after I complete it, I feel the equal of Itzhak Perlman or Joshua Bell. What a thrill!

I look forward to continuing my musical training at Yale, where I plan to audition for your orchestra's string section. By joining this talented group of teachers and musicians, I will have a once-in-a-lifetime opportunity to expand the limits of my musical talent. My only request is a roommate who appreciates the constant practice of an obsessive, but lighthearted violinist. If that's not possible, can you direct me to a store that sells ear plugs?

Our Assessment: The candidate used the same essay for questions about her favorite hobby and outside activity. By using a healthy dose of humor, she revealed her fun-loving personality, which her reference letters also confirmed.

Factors that Shaped Your Identity   (Common Application: 750 word limit)

Every day, after the final bell at school, I ran to the convenience store in downtown Cicero that my parents owned and operated. Between four and midnight, I served a steady stream of customers who bought gas, snack food, and lottery tickets on their way to (and from) work. To my younger siblings, this was a thankless job with few intrinsic rewards. Yet, to me, our successful business was proof of our family's ability to build a successful life in America. By working hard and watching our finances, my parents managed to purchase a home, launch their business, and support our large extended family in India. As a result, I was convinced that I would enjoy a comparable level of success by following their example.

Unfortunately, due to the demands of the store, my parents viewed my work there as a higher priority than my education. Consequently, I often skipped classes and worked late into the night when my father was short-handed. Everything changed in 2009, when he collapsed at the store and died from a heart attack. In subsequent days, we learned that the trappings of success that we had enjoyed were all an illusion; beyond the assets in the store, there was no money or life insurance to pay our ongoing expenses. Instead, we were forced to close the store and sell the inventory for pennies on the dollar. A year later, we moved into a homeless shelter when the bank foreclosed on the home that my parents had worked so hard to buy.

This life-changing event taught me a powerful lesson in humility. In an instant, we went from successful entrepreneurs to grieving survivors who relied upon public assistance. Although I was grateful for the help that we received, I was determined to acquire the education I would need to support my family and serve as an example for others. Balancing a job with the demands of my classes presented formidable time and logistical challenges. Nevertheless, I was determined to set a positive example for my siblings by handling them with grace and dignity.

I also discovered that my family's problems were far from unique. In our minority neighborhood, formal education is rarely a priority. As a result, few children have the academic training and practical experience they need to make wise decisions about their future. Like many children from immigrant families, I struggled to succeed in an educational system with which my parents were not familiar. Fortunately, I had a strong support system in Cicero's Indian-American community, which kept me focused on my long-term goals.

Next month, I will proudly graduate as the valedictorian of my 300-member high school class. I have also received scholarship awards from the YWCA, the Elk Society, and the Middle Eastern Academic Symposium. I would never have received these honors without the support of my family, friends, teachers, and mentors, who had tremendous faith in my ability to create a better future. They also ignited my desire to share the benefits of my education with those who have not enjoyed similar opportunities. Far too often, the kids in my neighborhood are forced to drop out of school in order to support their families. Without the benefits of a college degree, they cannot obtain a good job or build a successful life. As someone who was fortunate enough to escape a dead-end existence, I am determined to pave a clear path for others to do the same.

Today, because of my support system, I have escaped the temptations of drugs and violence that plague the streets of Cicero. Most importantly, I have realized that education is the only path to a safe and successful future, in which there truly are no limits. After college, I hope to pursue a graduate degree in social work, followed by a career as an inner city counselor. By doing so, I can find practical ways to transform communities through the power of a positive example. At the very least, I can encourage other children to stay in school and fulfill their academic potential.

Our Assessment: The candidate used the same essay to answer a question about his long-term goals and an obstacle he overcame. By positioning himself as a survivor (rather than a victim), he gained considerable respect from the reader, who knew that he had the strength and tenacity to help others succeed.

Factors that Shaped Your Identity   (600 word limit)

As the fifth of seven children, I have been fortunate to be surrounded by an encouraging family throughout my entire life. Their loyalty and support have enabled me to overcome several obstacles, including my difficult transition to life in the United States. As a traditional Hindu, I have struggled to balance the divergent aspects of the American and Indian cultures. My brothers helped me to create my own unique personality.

After our relocation to the US, my siblings also helped me to adjust to the absence of our father, who chose to remain in Bangalore. To compensate for his absence, my four older brothers took the initiative to fill the paternal role in my life. Their generosity ultimately made me a more selfless person. To share my blessings with others, I devote my free time to the Indian Wellness Center in lower Manhattan, which serves the needs of poor and struggling immigrants. During busy times, simply answering the phones and cleaning the office can give their staffers a much-needed break.

Along with selflessness, the trust and support from my family has also given me self-confidence. Unlike those who fear making mistakes and looking foolish, I am always eager to try new things and experiment with different ideas. I have not been successful in every endeavor, but I have learned the limits of my talent. Whether I succeed or fail in anyone else's eyes, I am a winner simply by taking the initiative to learn more about myself. Few of my peers enjoy a comparable level of confidence.

How much do I trust my family? With my life. When I was ten years old, I got lost on the subway in the heart of New York City. Somehow, I became separated from my older brother and missed my planned stop. By the time I got off the subway, I was in the heart of Bensonhurst, where no one spoke a word of English. Rather than panic, I simply kept in mind my brother's advice, "If you are ever lost or in trouble, go to the police." I flagged down a passing taxi, which brought me to the nearest police station in Brooklyn.

In the busy hallway, my brother Ankur anxiously paced the floor. Thankfully, he immediately realized that I had missed my stop and gotten stuck on the subway until Bensonhurst. When he couldn't find me himself, Ankur automatically went to the police station to get assistance. This is just one example of the amazing connection that I have with my six brothers. Alone in a new city, among seven million complete strangers, I was certain that Ankur would find me…….and he did.

When they hear the story, my friends always ask me what I would have done if Ankur had not been waiting for me at the police station. With such a large family, I had several options. Perhaps I would have called my mother and asked her to pick me up. Or, I could have left her a message to pass on to Ankur about my whereabouts. Or perhaps I would have called my older brother, who was attending college at Columbia University. Whatever choice I made, I knew that I would be found, loved and treasured. That is the gift that my family has given me, and it is what I have to offer other people.

Perhaps the greatest thing about family loyalty is that it isn't confined to my blood relatives. In fact, it is contagious. By instilling in me the trust, loyalty and self-confidence that they have received from our parents, my brothers have inspired me to share my blessings with my friends, my school and my community. At Harvard, I sincerely hope to provide the campus community with the same type of acceptance and love that has meant so much to me.

Our Assessment: This essay about the candidate's family started off the same as many others. The most memorable aspect is the story about getting lost on the subway and following his brother's advice to go to the police station. That anecdote brought the author's essay to life and proved the strong connection he had with his family. It is an excellent example of "showing" the reader a relationship, rather than "telling" them about it.

Factors that Shaped Your Identity   (Common Application: 750 word limit)

When I look at my freshman class picture, I realize how much I have grown in the past three years. Less than one month after the photograph was taken, I moved across the United States, which forced me to begin my sophomore year at Washburn High School in Bend, Oregon. At fourteen, I endured the stigma of being not just the "new kid in town," but "lower-middle class" in a decidedly upscale community. On an emotional level, I was completely unprepared for the move. At the time, the most important things in my world were the Chicago White Sox and the latest sequel to "Jurassic Park." Even my t-shirt in the photo has the logo of Navy Pier, which revealed my loyalty to the city I had always called home. After a lifetime of experiences along the Magnificent Mile, I couldn't imagine how I would survive in rural Bend.

In retrospect, moving cross-country was a life-changing experience for me, although I resisted the process for many months. From day one, Washburn High School was a startling contrast to my old school, Cicero High. At Washburn, education was paramount. The few jocks on campus weren't treated like gods the way they would have been in Chicago. In such a dedicated environment, the classroom became a whole different realm. In Chicago, the teachers preached the importance of learning, but it was obvious that the most important concern was grades. At Washburn, the teachers genuinely believed that learning was the most important objective. Consequently, they encouraged us to collaborate and share our resources.

In fact, in my senior literature class, my teacher assigned us a different non-fiction book each week. The only requirement was that we expand our intellectual horizons by choosing titles and subject areas that were outside our "comfort zone." As a result, I know more about decorating, past-life regression, bread making, tarot cards and WordPerfect than I could ever have imagined. Teaching methods like this, which encourage independent reading and continual learning, are an excellent preparation for my future in information technology. I have especially come to appreciate the focus on thinking, rather than memorization. Whether in English class or Math lab, I must approach every idea creatively, rather than simply regurgitate the teacher's words. In my discussions with other students, both inside and outside of class, we are amazed by the solutions we find simply by pooling our own ideas.

On a personal level, my greatest achievement has been living away from my parents during the school year, while I stay with my aunt and uncle. By adapting not only to a new city and school, but to a new family, I was forced to become my own person at a very young age. My school principal has been extremely helpful in my gradual growth to adulthood. In his own words, "Character can be measured not by one's interaction with people who are better off than him or herself, but by one's interactions with those who are worse off." By sharing my resources with others, however limited they may be, I have not only become a stronger person, but an integral part of the community. This past year, I came full-circle by serving as a Senior Guide to a new freshman girl from Costa Rica. At first glance, Maria and I are nothing alike, but we share the trauma of having to adapt to a dramatically new environment. By helping her find her niche, I am giving back to the community that has nurtured me so well over the past three years.

As I apply to colleges across the US, I am grateful to the people in Bend and Chicago who have taught me that "my place" is wherever I choose to make it. Although I am very different from the shy girl in my freshman class picture, I have managed to retain the traits that best define who I am. I still love the Chicago White Sox and sci-fi movies, and I wouldn't dream of missing a chance to visit the Second City Comedy Troupe. But I also have a place in my heart for the people, places and experiences in Bend, which are stimulating and precious in their own right.

Our Assessment: The strength of this essay is that the author acknowledges the important ways that both Bend and Chicago have shaped the woman she has become. She also shows keen insight into the different educational styles at the schools she has attended – and her own preference for a collaborative style that gives her the freedom to explore her own interests.

Factors that Shaped Your Identity   **(500 word limit)**

As a young boy in Brooklyn, I was crazy about the New York Yankees. I followed every game on television and radio, paying close attention to the play-by-play commentary. At age six, during my first trip to Yankee Stadium, I watched Ron Guidry pitch a game for the very first time. He quickly became my hero, both for his amazing ability to throw a curveball and for his obvious love of baseball. After watching him dazzle a stadium of 20,000 rapturous fans, I couldn't imagine a better role model.

Looking back, I favored the flamboyant Guidry over the less famous players because of his ability to energize the crowd. From my childish perspective, he was like a firecracker that could go off at any moment, striking out his competitors at an inconceivable pace. A media darling, Guidry won five straight Gold Glove awards, along with the coveted Cy Young Award. Once, after an unexpected victory, he left the field to play the drums with the Backstreet Boys. At that time in my life, sports were mostly for entertainment. Competing to win was secondary to the dazzling show that Ron Guidry put on.

After years of watching and playing competitive sports, I now view athletics quite differently. Unfortunately, despite my passion for the game, I never shared Guidry's ability to strike out batters or hit a grand slam home run. Yet I thoroughly enjoyed playing on my high school softball team. Some of my headiest memories involve the adrenaline rush that accompanied a great hit and the lump in my throat when we unexpectedly lost. Even when my team was outmatched, I took great pride in fighting a good fight and exceeding my own standards.

Although my primary goal was recreation, sports ultimately taught me a lot about working on a team. Even with a "star" player, the game was rarely won or lost by just one person's skills. Keeping the other team at bay required split-second timing and collaboration; every man in the outfield had a vital job to do. Likewise, when the going was tough, it was the persistence of my teammates that kept me going. We gelled together as a cohesive unit by playing to our strengths and concealing our weaknesses. Although I was thrilled by our hard-fought wins, the true victory was in our special camaraderie.

In team events, a maverick like Ron Guidry is no longer my idea of a hero. Looking back, his priority was not helping his team mates, but in promoting his own career. Although there is a place for showmanship in athletics, the need for restraint and controlled aggression is equally important. Today, in all aspects of life, my heroes are the clutch performers who play within their limitations, but push their potential within that framework to achieve the team's objectives. They may not be the most graceful or talented players, but they come through when the team needs them most. They are the unsung heroes behind every so-called "superstar."

Our Assessment: This essay is unique because it cites the author's hero in the first paragraph, then explains how he lost respect for that person as he grew up. By including examples from his own softball career, the candidate makes a persuasive case for his new definition of a hero.

Factors that Shaped Your Identity   (500 word limit)

Although my mother calls me a dreamer, I prefer to see myself as an agent of social change. Perhaps naively, I believe that if enough people on this earth champion a cause, we can reverse our downward spiral of poverty, depression and despair. Caring is just the first step, however. People must act on their ideals by working together to achieve the social reforms that are necessary for our collective survival. After examining the many worthy causes in need of support, I have opted to focus my energy in the reform of feminism.

Why feminism? The obvious answer is because I am a woman, which makes me keenly aware of the subtle forms of discrimination that continue to plague my sex. Another reason is my deep-rooted sense of justice, which inspires me to fight on behalf of those who are placed at an unfair disadvantage. But the primary reason is that I am courageous enough to handle the many challenges and obstacles that being a feminist presents. Every cause needs a champion who is fearless; thankfully, the feminist movement has me.

Inspired by a personal meeting with Gloria Steinem, I decided to start a young feminist club at John F. Kennedy High School to address issues regarding gender equality. We organized an assembly to raise awareness about women's issues and to dispel the myths surrounding feminism. We also held a car wash to benefit Planned Parenthood and participated in many Pro-Choice rallies and marches. Over the past four years, I have spent much of my free time volunteering for local activist groups, such as the Bristol County Abused Women's Services and the Providence Chapter of the National Organization for Women. Through my work on feminist causes, I have promoted important social issues that are usually ignored by our male-dominated legislatures.

My other social activities have given me invaluable experience in the political and judicial world. By participating in Mock Trial, I have argued difficult cases in front of a real judge. As a result, I have learned much about the legal system and my own personal rights. I also enjoy serving as a delegate for the Model United Nations. By taking a position on a particular political economic or social issue - and debating it with those who assume alternative perspectives – I have learned how the policies that affect the global community are made.

Throughout my work on behalf of feminist causes, I have continued to participate in other social activities to retain a sense of balance in my life. I especially enjoy creative writing, such as plays and poems, and I work as the Features Editor on the school paper. I also play on my school's varsity lacrosse team. My various activities have taught me many things about myself and my place in the world. Most importantly, I have learned that I must work to change the world, without ever abandoning my sense of humor. Nothing can be taken too seriously, not even myself.

Our Assessment: This candidate has won several awards for her Mock Trial experience, which revealed her impressive skills as a debater. In this essay, she reveals her passion for feminism – and the spirit of equality that the term suggests. After reading it, the committee knew that she would be a welcome addition to programs that would allow her to continue to cultivate her skills as a speaker, writer, and advocate.

International Travel   (500 word limit)

Last fall, I participated in a humanitarian mission trip that literally transformed my life. I accompanied five members of the International Red Cross team to Darfur, where we assisted civilians who were displaced by the war between the government and the non-Arab indigenous population. Upon my arrival, I witnessed the ongoing threats that the residents endure, including poverty, disease, malnutrition, and random violence. On my first day, a military official showed us how to identify, extract, and de-activate a landmine. He also explained how to protect ourselves if we encountered an armed terrorist. These experiences showed me the daily reality of the locals, who were trapped in a violent world in which the danger was impossible to predict.

The following day, we distributed dry rations, new clothes, and school supplies at an orphanage that housed more than 100 survivors of the recent violence. A number of the children I met had lost not only their homes, but their entire family. It was humbling to know that the supplies we delivered, including vitamins, antibiotics, and bandages, could be used to save a life.

Throughout our trip, we spent considerable time traveling among the various facilities that needed our help. After our trip to the orphanage, we visited a makeshift Red Cross Hospital in Darfur, which had been destroyed by several terrorist attacks. Along the way, we stopped at camps that provided temporary shelter for people who were displaced by the civil war. According to our team leader, who had visited the same camps a year before, hundreds of occupants had already found permanent rehabilitation. However, we also spoke to several people who were still waiting for a safe place to live, and were forced to stay in overcrowded camps that lack clean water, healthy food, sanitary conditions, and security. Not surprisingly, in this unhealthy and impoverished environment, few people have hope for a safe future.

In our free time, we helped our host family with their small farming business, which bore little resemblance to the industrial facilities in developed nations. With no money, machinery, or fertilizer, the farmers in Darfur rely upon rain, hard work, and the power of their cattle to plough the soil. Their yield, of course, is dependent upon the amount of rainfall the area receives; during times of drought, the farmers barely make enough money to survive. As I watched them work, I was amazed by their ability to move quickly and easily through the thick mud. The volunteers, in contrast, struggled to take a single step in these intense conditions. When I removed my boots at the end of the day, I had a newfound appreciation for the labor required to harvest a single grain of rice.

On my long ride home, I realized how blessed I am to live in a safe home with a loving family that has the physical, financial, and emotional support to face life's challenges. In contrast, the people in Darfur, though no fault of their own, struggle arduously simply to survive. By volunteering for the International Red Cross, I fulfilled my desire to visit a part of my continent that had been completely alien to me. As summer begins, I am eager to visit the region again, to continue the work for such a noble cause. Surely, during my years at Columbia, I can convince my fellow students to support similar humanitarian initiatives, which serve the needs of deserving residents of the war-torn regions of Sudan and other countries.

<u>Our Assessment</u>: This essay revealed the candidate's observations of a war-torn area, where the residents struggle simply to survive. His commitment to helping them, which is confirmed in the final paragraph of his essay, confirms that this trip made a lasting impact on his life.

International Travel   (600 word limit)

Long before my birth, my mother taught calculus at the Russian Embassy School in Moscow. From my earliest memory, she has encouraged me to study mathematics to better understand the nature of life. I was immediately attracted to the perfection of mathematics and its underlying dichotomy. On one hand, the discipline was entirely created by man; as a result, the rules could easily be shaped to suit a mathematician's needs. On the other hand, the rules of logic are the final judge, which means there can be no differing opinions. Beginning in the second grade, I explored these concepts by participating in several after-school clubs and competitions. Eventually, in the fourth grade, I earned a full scholarship to the Hunter Academy, which is a prestigious school in Moscow that specialized in mathematics.

When my family moved to the United States five years ago, it became harder for me to pursue my mathematical interests. Despite my passion for numbers, my English was poor and my parents lacked the financial resources to enroll me in a private school. Nevertheless, I made it to the national round of the American Mathematics Competition (AMC) during my freshman year. As a sophomore, I participated in a Westinghouse quantitative talent search competition, in which I placed third on the national level. The coordinator invited me to attend their summer Young Scholars Program, where I learned to develop my problem solving skills. Finally, this year, I organized a Mathletes team to compete in local and regional competitions.

In hindsight, my passion for mathematics helped me to adjust to my new culture. Without conversational fluency in English, I felt uncomfortable in my history and government classes, which required a working knowledge of the language. In math class, however, I was immersed in the universal language of numbers, in which I have always been fluent. By participating in the AMC competition, I surrounded myself with other kindred souls (ie geeks), who share my love of all things quantitative. With each new achievement in math, I feel a closer bond with my mother, whose talent in the field is unsurpassed.

Thanks to the generosity of my parents, I have also been able to nurture my love of computers. In 2009, we actually bought a new laptop rather than take a winter vacation. After teaching myself several programming languages, including Pascal, C, and C++, I was invited to attend Cornell University's Center for Talented Youth program, where I completed a course entitled Data Structures and Algorithms. And last year, as a member of the Engineering Club, I used my knowledge of computers and programming to help design a new interface for a shopping cart program for online auctions.

When my family decided to move here in 2006, I was wary of the many obstacles that would accompany an international relocation. As a shy thirteen-year-old, I did not understand the many ways that moving to America would enhance my life. To an outsider, the primary benefits are the nation's unlimited professional and educational opportunities. Yet, for me, the greatest benefit of moving to the US from Russia has been my exposure to people with other backgrounds and preferences. Although my accent occasionally elicits ignorant remarks, having a multicultural background has had an overwhelmingly positive effect on my life. By assimilating into a melting pot, I opened my mind to new possibilities and developed friendships that transcend racial, cultural and religious lines. I am eager to pursue my undergraduate degree at Harvard, whose diverse population sparks a level of creativity that cannot exist in a cultural vacuum.

Our Assessment: This author successfully explains how her multicultural background has expanded her perspective and given her the confidence to build relationships with different types of people. At the same time, she documents her lifetime love of science and mathematics, which are her intended areas of specialization.

International Travel   (Common Application: 750 word limit)

In September of 2008, my father accepted a one-year assignment with the South American Wildlife Federation, which was headquartered in rural Brazil. After careful consideration, he decided that this cross-cultural experience was something that my mother and I simply should not miss. So, on a crisp fall day, we boarded a plane in New York City that took us to the outskirts of Itabuna, Brazil.

From the start, I was fascinated by the language, history, and people of this exotic place. During the first few months of our stay, we toured ancient cathedrals in Salvador and sunbathed in the pristine beaches in Ilheus. While navigating the Amazon River, we watched wild animals migrate across the lush rain forest, completely oblivious to our presence. During our relaxing weekends, as we swam and hiked along the water, we marveled at the natural beauty that Brazil had to offer.

Everything changed in late December, when my uncle decided to visit us for a month. Upon his arrival, he shared several intriguing stories with us about his Peace Corps experience in Brazil a decade earlier. The sharp contrast between the simple lifestyle that my uncle described and the one I was enjoying showed me how un-Brazilian my adventure really was. Although I was in a foreign country, I attended an American-run, English-speaking school that was populated by mostly European and Asian students. Our thriving section of Itabuna had numerous shopping malls, ethnic restaurants and movie theaters that catered to our wealthy group of expatriates. After talking to my uncle, I asked myself a painful question: was this really the true essence of the Amazon?

Upon reflection, I realized that my daily activities were almost the same as they were in the United States. I typed my homework papers on a computer; I showered with hot water after soccer practice; and I dined on hamburgers, hot dogs and fried chicken. Thanks to my father's position, I was part of a tight-knit group of expatriates who managed to retain all of the luxuries of my American lifestyle. The problem was that I wasn't really seeing Brazil. Before I left the country, I yearned to experience the authentic Brazilian culture without sacrificing my education.

My uncle's extended holiday trip provided the perfect solution. After talking it over with my parents, he agreed to take me along for a two-week jaunt to deliver health care supplies to a family in rural Zanzibar. We would travel by car to the remote mountainous location and sleep in the family's small clay hut. Although the conditions sounded primitive, I was up for the challenge. This excursion proved to be the most rewarding ten days of my entire stay in Brazil. In that short period, I learned more about Brazilian culture than I had in the previous three months.

On my first day, I witnessed how hard Brazilian women were expected to work to maintain the efficiency of the household. They had to cook the meals, get the milk, sweep the house, chop the firewood and take care of the children. Although the men did some hunting, they mostly enjoyed a laid-back lifestyle. I also saw an intense restlessness for change. When the men sat around the dinner table, they did not discuss the weather or the latest village gossip. Instead, they debated the social and economic problems in Brazil and what could be done to improve their country. They voiced their apprehension about the government, their fear of inflation and the deleterious effects of cocaine production in the region. And, increasingly, the residents worried about the increasing drug use among their nation's youth. Unwilling to accept defeat, these men were hungry for the solutions that education and money could bring.

Despite the lack of amenities, I discovered that their primitive lifestyle was not necessarily a painful one. Over time, people adjusted to a lack of running water, electricity, telephones and cars. Although their days were filled with physical labor, their evenings were filled with the joy and companionship of their families and friends. Each night in Zanzibar, we ate good food, the children played and the adults enjoyed lively conversation. Although their lifestyle was vastly different from mine, we shared the common goals of education, happiness and success.

After the New Year, when I returned to my parents' home in Itabuna, I realized that I had finally found what I was looking for. Thanks to my two weeks in Zanzibar, I had gained a true understanding of rural Brazil, along with the satisfaction of experiencing something beyond the American expatriate community.

Our Assessment: The strength of this essay is the author's realization that he was not seeing the true Brazilian lifestyle during his time in Ilheus. Rather than enjoy his material blessings, he took the initiative to explore a rural part of the nation, which enjoyed few modern amenities. Although many candidates write similar essays each year, this one was particularly sincere, detailed, and memorable.

International Travel   (300 word limit)

"Do you travel on elephants? Wear a turban on your head? Are there tigers roaming the streets?" When I arrived in New Hampshire to attend high school, I was astonished by people's ignorance about Middle Eastern culture. Suddenly, I was not only the "new girl" in school, but the only person of Indian descent that my peers had ever known. Every day, I found myself bombarded by questions that were silly, intrusive and downright insulting. Sadly, although I had welcomed the opportunity to study abroad, I began to question my decision. For several weeks, I felt depressed and isolated in the New England countryside.

To improve my sense of belonging, I began to talk with other international students about their diverse life experiences. I also began to use a few local expressions so I could blend in with the crowd. Soon, I befriended a diverse group of students who shared my interests in rugby, cricket and business. Through the Student Business Club and the India Club, I pondered new business ideas and kept abreast of other cultures. I also worked on several international project teams that helped me to improve my interpersonal and teamwork skills.

Yet my first months in the United States were primarily a time of growth and experimentation. As an exchange student, I was challenged by my need to support myself financially, which did not always leave a lot of time to study. Although my grades suffered because of my hectic schedule, I learned how to manage my time and juggle multiple responsibilities. At a young age, I also became independent enough to thrive in an international environment.

Once I adjusted to life in New Hampshire, I used the comments about tigers, jungles and grass huts as an opportunity to educate my new friends about the fascinating history, culture and languages of India. By doing so, I opened their hearts and minds to people, places and perspectives they would never have learned about any other way. Hopefully, I also diffused any lingering concerns that lions, tigers, and elephants roamed the streets of Bangalore.

Our Assessment: This candidate used the same essay to answer questions about a challenging life experience and as an addendum to explain her disappointing GPA. To us, its primary strength is its introduction and closing, which listed the many questions she was forced to answer during her first days in New Hampshire. For readers who had survived similar experiences, it struck a familiar chord.

International Travel   **(500 word limit)**

For many people, cooking is a nightly burden with few intrinsic rewards. When pressed for time, they are happy to grab a hamburger at McDonalds or pop a frozen pizza in the oven. Yet, for many generations of my family, cooking has provided a cherished social occasion to create and enjoy the most delectable dishes.

My passion for preparing gourmet meals stems from my fond memories of childhood dinners in my parents' household in Budapest. On Saturday morning, my mother asked for our input for Sunday dinner. Then, we spent the day procuring fresh ingredients at the Farmer's Market, where the smell of fresh produce permeated the air. After buying seasonal vegetables, we created delightful blends of international meals, including spicy beef kebab (a regional specialty) and Hungarian zucchini pancakes. Although these dishes took hours to prepare, once we sat down at the dinner table and began to discuss our day, the memory of our hard work dissipated into animated chatter and laughter.

Aside from my appreciation for good food, I never gave cooking much thought until I moved to the United States at age 14 to spend a year with my host family. My initial adjustment to a steady diet of "convenience foods" was agonizing. Instead of the tasty dinners I enjoyed at my parents' home, we ate hamburgers, hot dogs, and an occasional ready-mix chili. Even worse, my host family's spice drawer was collecting dust and their kitchen cabinets were filled with canned goods, which were a major taboo in my parents' home.

Although I occasionally enjoyed fast food, I was not fond of eating it on a daily basis. Fortunately, my host family's busy lifestyle gave me the chance to show off my culinary skills. With my host mother's help, I took the initiative to create nice home-cooked meals from different cultures. Ultimately, we both benefited from this experience; while I learned how to prepare American specialties like apple pie and Thanksgiving turkey, she learned how to make feta cheese pastries and a traditional potato salad.

After I graduated from high school, I attended the prestigious Le Cordon Bleu in London, where I combined my passion for cooking with my love for the hospitality industry. By attending classes in Wine History and Desserts Merchandising, I further sharpened my culinary knowledge and cooking skills. Thanks to my creative flair, I quickly developed a reputation for being a whiz in the kitchen. While most of my peers skimmed the necessary textbook chapters, I meticulously read the material and experimented with new recipes. In my spare time, I followed the trends of my favorite television chefs and re-created their most enticing concoctions.

Although I no longer work as a chef, cooking remains a major part of my life. Living in a culinary mecca like New York, I am continually inspired to try new things. Whenever possible, I flaunt my skills by entertaining my friends with creative dinner party themes. Their full bellies and effusive compliments strengthen my belief that good times are always enhanced by good food.

Our Assessment: This delightful essay covers several themes effectively, including the candidate's multicultural background, love of cooking, and professional experience as a chef. By presenting her experiences honestly and creatively, she distinguished herself from other candidates who wrote "fish out of water" stories.

International Travel   **(300 word limit)**

As the daughter of a U.S. diplomat, I spent three years in Frankfurt, Germany, where I attended an international school that enrolled students from 30 different countries. The experience changed my life in countless ways. From the minute I stepped off the plane in Frankfurt, the vastly different sights along the roads and the smells of delicious German cuisine told me that I was "not in Kansas anymore." My school also helped to expand my world view, as I found myself studying with students from countries I had previously only read about. Although it was sometimes difficult to relate to my British, Zambian, or Chilean friends, I soon came to enjoy my new environment. By the time I left, I wondered how I ever could survive the boredom of attending a homogeneous institution.

My understanding of my new home was aided tremendously by my ability to speak French and German, which were the best gifts I brought back from my stay in Europe. An entire year of school lessons could not have taught me as much of the language as I learned from speaking with my friends, shopping in the local stores, and taking music lessons at the local conservatory. My proficiency in French earned me a regular spot on a nationally broadcast radio program, in which a Russian student and I discussed the tensions between the major world powers. This was a rare opportunity for me to explore "hot topics" with someone my own age, who had first-hand knowledge about post-Cold War Russia. Beforehand, I had never explored such a controversial topic in such depth and passion.

Thanks to my three years in Germany, the United States will never seem the same to me. By immersing myself in a dramatically different culture, I gained enough distance from America to view it more objectively. In my quieter moments, I acknowledged my country's numerous faults, as well as its unparalleled strengths. I also came to appreciate the beauty and culture of Germany, which had provided me with a rich, unique, and stimulating adolescence.

Our Assessment: This essay, although short, explains the many ways the candidate benefitted from living and studying in Europe. It also complemented the material in her primary essay, which discussed her work as a language tutor in the US. When taken together, the two essays gave the reader a true understanding of the candidate's ability to add value to a heterogeneous educational environment.

Diversity   (500 word limit)

Compared to my high school in mainland China, the John F. Kennedy Academy in New York City is an organization with a completely different persona. When I first arrived on campus, I experienced what people call "culture shock." Fortunately, I am the type of person who can easily adapt to different environments. In less than six months, I have not only adjusted to American culture, but developed a sense of humor about its oddities.

One of the first things I noticed after setting foot on U.S. soil is that Americans, the residents of New York City in particular, are more law-abiding than the Chinese. Here, drivers do not run through red lights or flood the pavement with their motorcycles. Also, people throw their garbage in the bin, rather than along the roads. In China, nothing is as organized or pristine as the streets of lower Manhattan.

In terms of character, Americans and Chinese are like a north and a south pole. While Americans tend to speak what is on their mind, Chinese do not. Even when we are angry, sad, or annoyed, we won't express our real feelings. Rather than hurt other people, we prefer to suppress our emotions. As a result, people cannot tell what a Chinese person is thinking from his or her facial expression. In this respect, we are as skilled as Hollywood's best actors and actresses. There is even an old Chinese proverb that says (loosely translated), "What is said is different from what is thought." A Chinese person can give you the sweetest smile you have ever seen, while he is actually so angry that he wants to stab you to death.

Clothing is also a visible difference between the two groups. Americans tend to dress casually, particularly at JFK Academy, where there is no dress code. Most of the teachers wear sports shirts and jeans; only a few dress in suits. The students dress even more casually; in order to save time, some even roll out of bed and come to class wearing their pajamas. In contrast, the teachers and professors in China all wear suits, while the students are required to wear school uniforms or collared-shirts. Flip-flops are prohibited; students are only allowed to wear polished black shoes with matching socks.

As I adapt to life in America, I will undoubtedly notice additional differences between China and the U.S. That is why I am eager to live in several different countries. By experiencing other cultures, I will broaden my horizons and find new ways to look at things. Although, personally, I will never be so "laid back" that I will wear my pajamas to school.

Our Assessment: This essay, which makes several obvious comparisons between China and the US, is also quite funny. The author clearly has a sense of humor about both cultures, which came through loud and clear in her writing.

Diversity   (500 word limit)

Popular cliches about "appearances being deceiving" are particularly relevant to those of multi-cultural heritage. By appearance, I am a stereotypical Indian male, with dark hair, olive skin and a lean, athletic build. Yet my childhood in Barrington, Illinois has been decidedly "American," which has provided a powerful contrast to my parents' lives in Bangalore. As a result, I have spent seventeen years bridging the gap between two very different cultures and carving out an identity that is uniquely my own.

After leaving their native India, my parents embraced life in the United States for the myriad educational and professional opportunities that it affords. From my earliest memories, my parents have encouraged me to do everything possible to succeed, yet their unfamiliarity with the American culture placed me at a distinct disadvantage when I started elementary school. Guided by my strict Indian upbringing, I had a difficult time finding my place in a culture that celebrates sports icons and MTV, rather than religious or community leaders.

With a burgeoning Indian and Asian population, Barrington eventually became more tolerant of ethnic diversity. Yet, throughout my early childhood, my parents and I simultaneously struggled to integrate ourselves into mainstream society. My greatest challenge was gaining acceptance into a peer group whose values were inherently superficial. Even as a young child, I knew that other parents did not share my family's focus on education.

Academia became my salvation. With a proclivity for math and science, I became one my school's most popular "computer jocks." I brought honor to the school by winning second place in the national competition in Technology Concepts, which was sponsored by the Future Business Leaders of America. Later, by participating on the school newspaper and the Model UN, I found my niche among a group of academically-gifted students. Ironically, as I became more confident of my identity, I was more selective in seeking friends. Several of the most popular students at my school were intolerant of diversity. Rather than welcome new perspectives, they tormented those who they perceived to be "different." Some of their actions, which were fueled by fear and ignorance, were cruel and morally wrong. Rather than turn a blind eye, I adhered to my core values and surrounded myself with compassionate friends who are more accepting of others.

As I prepare for college, I embrace the benefits of my dual heritage, which allows me to appreciate Indian chants and alternative rock in equal measure. Both cultural influences have shaped my character and made me the independent thinker I am today. With my strong intellectual curiosity, I am eager to enroll in a top-notch computer science program to prepare for a career as a software engineer. A talented pianist and basketball player, I will also pursue opportunities to develop my athletic and musical potential. On a campus that celebrates diversity, the enrichment possibilities will be endless. Throughout my endeavors, I will continue to share my success with my parents, who have encouraged me to fulfill my educational dream. After all, their vision of a better life in America was the catalyst to everything I have achieved.

Our Assessment: This essay stands out because the author had the confidence to address a "dirty little secret" regarding diversity; in many places, there is blatant discrimination against those who look, talk, and act differently than the norm. This candidate had the confidence to stand up for other students who faced ignorance and hatred in his school. By doing so, he proved that he is not only a kind and accepting young man, but a true leader.

Diversity   (Common Application: 750 word limit)

The sun was just setting as I arrived at work on a Friday evening in August. I quickly threw on my Baskin Robbins apron to assist my coworkers.

"Can I have a double scoop of chocolate mocha with butterscotch sauce, please?"

I rang up the ice cream and handed an empty cup to LaDawna, our 24-year-old shift leader. Two scoops of chocolate mocha, a squirt of butterscotch sauce, and the customer's order was ready. After she left, LaDawna began to chat as we cleaned the counter tops.

With college applications looming, LaDawna asked me where I wanted to go to school. My short answer "Columbia" brought slight confusion to her face.

"Is that a good school?" she asked.

"Yes, it's an excellent place," I responded, as LaDawna sighed with relief. I realized that she wasn't familiar with Columbia, despite its close proximity and great reputation.

"Well, good luck, Tina. I wish I had the opportunity to go to college."

Questions began to swirl in my mind. What did she mean? Why didn't she have the opportunity? There were several colleges within twenty miles of our store. Why didn't she take the time to earn a degree? Her answers shocked me.

"My mother died of cancer when I was eight and my father abandoned us shortly afterwards. My brother and I lived in eight different foster homes by the time I was seventeen. I never had time to study. Heck, I never stayed in one place long enough to make friends."

With a slight shrug and an embarrassed smile, LaDawna stopped talking. For a few moments, we suffered in awkward silence. Despite our superficial friendship, I realized that I didn't "know" LaDawna at all. Although she acted like a carefree teenager, LaDawna had been working full-time since she was seventeen. Through no fault of her own, she was denied all of the carefree moments of childhood that I had enjoyed. Her only family was a younger brother who was constantly in trouble with the law.

Until that moment, I didn't realize the profound differences between LaDawna's life and my own. We were both pretty, fun-loving, African-American girls from New York City who shared a love of hip hop, action movies, and beef lo mein. Yet, suddenly, I acknowledged a powerful difference between us that would ultimately determine our destinies. Despite working full-time for years, LaDawna had neither the money nor the time to pursue an education. She had no future other than Baskin Robbins. I felt guilty at the notion of leaving within a year and moving on to college.

Life isn't fair. Some of us are blessed with the intellect, the financial means, and the environment to succeed, while others never have a chance. My parents have always used the top-notch students in my school as paradigms. They claim that hard work can build a person into anyone or anything (s)he wants to be. Yet I know that this is not true. I have been given incredible blessings that are beyond the reach of many people. When I meet someone like LaDawna, I am reminded of my good fortune. My conscience warns me not to squander my opportunity to obtain an excellent education and fulfill my potential. As President John F. Kennedy advised, "To whom much is given, much is required."

Throughout my life, the people who have influenced me will remain in my memory and provide the motivation that I need to attain my goals. Many, like LaDawna, serve as powerful reminders of the fragility and randomness of life. No one knows why one person is blessed, while another is denied the basic essentials. Just one change in my family history (a divorce, accident, or untimely death) might have left me in LaDawna's shoes, facing challenges that are quite different from filling out college applications. With this in mind, I feel an extra motivation to pursue my dreams. Not everyone can.

The clock struck nine, and it was pitch dark outside. I punched out and headed home, leaving LaDawna to assist the next customer. She will never know how much I respect her.

Our Assessment: Many times, when we evaluate essays, we suggest that candidates *show* us something, rather than *tell* us about it. This essay uses the story about LaDawna to reveal the candidate's awareness and gratitude. It deeply touched every person who read it.

Diversity   (300 word limit)

After my parents divorced, my mother and I moved to the United States to ensure that I would receive an excellent education. Just three years old, I didn't realize the future challenges and rewards of being raised in a single-parent minority household. Without a formal education, my mother worked full-time as a waitress to pay for our food and rent. Home alone, I became proficient at making meals and cleaning the house. Although our life was difficult, we were blessed with the love and support from our family in China and our own close-knit relationship.

I studied diligently and excelled in school, despite our limited resources. Although my initial motivation was to honor my mother's sacrifices, I found myself increasingly intrigued by the complexities of the social sciences. At a young age, I wanted to understand that factors that influenced different societies and our own economic situation. During difficult times, I asked my mother, "Why did we leave China and come to the United States?" She answered, "Because there is freedom here." Unlike our homeland, where education was limited to a privileged few, America offered all residents a chance for social mobility and personal fulfillment. They simply needed to work hard and believe in themselves. What an incredible gift!

Despite my lack of material goods, my childhood taught me invaluable life lessons. I appreciate the fruit of my hard work and the little things that most people take for granted, such as good food and a comfortable home. I devour good books and reliable information, which are not readily available in most countries. But my greatest treasure is my mother, whose sacrifices will provide me will a happier and more fulfilling future than she ever acquired for herself. Ultimately, I want to use my knowledge and experience to empower other underprivileged children to pursue their own dreams. I cannot imagine a greater gift that I could give to the next generation.

<u>Our Assessment</u>: This essay is short, honest, and heartfelt, which is everything it needed to be. It also gives the reader a better understanding of what motivates the candidate to achieve her goals, which is to honor her mother's sacrifice.

Your Fit for a Particular School   **(Common Application: 750 word limit)**

As I prepare for my high school graduation, I am eager to select the right university. In my mind, the relationship between a student entering college is similar to that of a piece of iron being heated by a furnace; if the incoming quality is good, the end result will be exceptional. After visiting several schools and reviewing dozens of catalogs and web sites, I am confident that Princeton is an excellent fit for my skills and goals. As a prospective engineering major, I cannot imagine a better place to continue my education.

During my childhood in China, my parents strongly encouraged me to explore my diverse academic interests. On a trip to Germany, France, and England in 2005, I became intrigued by the scientific development and civilization of the Western world. As I explored my love of science, I realized that its advancements and breakthroughs required more than mastering theories and memorizing information. Throughout history, the true technical pioneers had to apply their knowledge to new and exciting situations.

Like a house, each scientific development is composed of thousands of "bricks" that provide support. Only by combining many ideas (or "bricks") in diverse fields can a scientist make his maximum contribution. Following my European trip, learning became my top priority, both inside and outside the classroom. In addition to my love for mathematics and physics, I also pursued my interest in literature, history and the social sciences. As I devoured books and articles on each topic, I realized the importance of eloquence and language. The best authors, regardless of their area of expertise, are effective communicators who present complex information in an understandable way. I am eager to develop the same skill. Rather than limit my studies to one specific area, I plan to acquire a rigorous, broad-based education that combines classes in math and science with those in the humanities.

When I moved to the United States in August of 2008, my love of learning helped me to brave the uncertainties of my new world. As I adjusted to a different culture, I was buoyed by the confidence I had developed from my earlier educational experiences. As a non-native speaker of English, I quickly addressed the critical issues regarding language and communication. By joining an Asian youth leadership club, I learned how to communicate effectively as a peer mentor. I later perfected my vocabulary and speaking skills through debate. Three years later, I have adapted well to my new surroundings and am fluent in both English and Mandarin.

I am continually intrigued by my classes in Physics, Calculus and Geometry, which explain the mathematical concepts and scientific principles of engineering. My interest in these areas is a reflection of my tendency to think logically and to use deductive reasoning to solve problems. As a science student, I love well-written textbooks that challenge my imagination and intellect. There is a beauty to mathematical concepts when they are presented in an orderly and intelligible way. During a meeting of the Junior Division of the American Chemical Society, I was surrounded by other students who shared my love of learning. I am excited by the prospect of attending college among a comparable group of talented and accomplished peers.

When I evaluated prospective colleges, I sought a place that had exceptional programs in mathematics, science and engineering, which are my true intellectual passions. At the same time, I wanted a school with strong departments in the humanities and social sciences, which will provide a sense of balance to my curriculum. Respected departments in English and communications were also essential, to enable me to perfect my skills as a writer, speaker and educator. After exhaustive research, I concluded that Princeton is the best place to fulfill my needs. Top notch academic programs, combined with an impressive selection of extracurricular activities, will allow me to learn and grow in an environment that encourages creativity and independent thinking. With my unique experiences, I will bring a fresh voice and an international viewpoint to all of my classroom discussions.

This essay is somewhat long, but reveals the unique strengths the candidate will bring to a top tier engineering program. By weaving several threads into the narrative, including his passion for science, his international travel experiences, and a difficult cultural adjustment, the candidate showed his confidence, flexibility, and continual desire to learn and grow.

Your Fit for a Particular School   (400 word limit)

My small, close-knit family is a constant source of love and inspiration. Although we have always enjoyed a nurturing relationship, the challenges we faced when we migrated from Ecuador to the United States brought us even closer. Whenever we faced a problem trying to assimilate into our new culture, we depended on each other for emotional support. My parents, who are both petroleum chemists, also provided the inspiration for me to join their profession. Watching them design safe and efficient oil rigs to fulfill our need for fossil fuels, I developed a strong passion for science and mathematics. At a young age, I began to read engineering textbooks to develop a better grasp of each topic. At age 14, I asked my parents, "Where is the best place to study petroleum chemistry and engineering?" They eagerly replied, "Stanford University. Although it is very competitive, it is an amazing place to get an education." Consequently, I have never even considered another school.

My life has also been shaped by my four years on the Pilgrim High School debate team, which helped me to transform from a quiet and shy girl into a mature and outspoken adult. By building and presenting arguments, I have honed my analytical skills and learned the importance of teamwork. I have also learned how to think on my feet and consider alternative ideas and perspectives. By conquering the trials and tribulations of debates, I have developed the maturity and confidence to succeed in the stimulating environment at Stanford.

Above all, I am a first-generation Ecuadorean-American, which has strongly influenced my career path. For the past several years, my country's educational system has been restructured to address the needs of a global economy. The increased focus on research and development is designed to provide students with the knowledge and skills they will need to innovate using cutting-edge technologies. I am eager to become part of this exciting field. As a petroleum chemist, I can channel my energy into a research-oriented industry with highly practical applications. I am passionate about studying at Stanford, where I will interact with talented teachers, researchers and scientists from across the globe. In such a rigorous environment, I can explore the limits of my potential and make my own contribution to the profession.

Legacy candidates face an unusual hurdle in the admissions process. On one hand, the committee looks favorably upon qualified candidates whose parents are alumni of the same school. On the other hand, they also want to know that the candidate has chosen the school on his/her own, without parental interference. In this essay, the candidate clearly expresses her love of science and engineering – and her desire to pursue a career that will benefit her native Ecuador. The essay was well perceived.

Your Fit for a Particular School   (400 word limit)

Despite my lifetime familiarity with Columbia, I did not appreciate my "fit" for the school until I spent time on campus during your 2011 Open House and Immersion Program. This unique experience was a magical time for me. As a Vietnamese-American, I seek a school with a diverse student body and a commitment to academic excellence. Columbia offers a chance for me to live and study in the heart of New York City, where I can interact with people from various cultures and walks of life.

After my birth in the United States, I attended a high school with less than 1% Asian students. As a result, my ethnic roots are sometimes unclear. Although my taste in music and film is decidedly American, my personality and values clearly reflect my Asian heritage; I respect my elders, excel in math and science, and enjoy a competitive and diligent nature. Deep in my heart, I often wonder if I am American, Asian or both. Columbia's Asian Pacific Student Coalition is a perfect opportunity for me to explore my ethnic roots and answer that question definitively.

As a future physician, I am particularly attracted to Columbia's commitment to scientific research. During Dr. Richard Smith's presentation, I learned about the university's renowned professors, unique academic characteristics and challenging dual degree programs. Since early childhood, I have dreamed of becoming a pediatrician who helps children recover from serious illnesses. A dual degree in biology and chemistry will prepare me for the rigors of medical school. With my aggressive nature and strong self-motivation, I welcome the challenges of a dual curriculum.

As a musician, my final enticement was the rhythmic chant of Columbia's marching band on a chilly Saturday morning. "Col-*um*-bi-a......Col-*um*-bi-a ... " As they marched across the quad, cheering for the football game against Penn, the band members inspired strong feelings of nostalgia. I longed for my days in the school band, when I relieved my stress by blowing into my saxophone. Through my training as a musician, I developed the self-discipline, patience, dedication and time management skills that continue to enrich my life. At Columbia, I will join the band's ceremonial march across the field, playing my beloved saxophone to showcase my school pride. When I march the field at halftime, I will share one of Columbia's richest, proudest, and most long-standing traditions.

Our Assessment: This candidate presented her answer to the "why us" question in the context of her experience at the school's open house. Every point gave the reader new information about her specific fit for what the university had to offer.

Your Fit for a Particular School   (400 word limit)

As a child, I was raised in a small town called Sproul, Pennsylvania, among a group of racially homogenous people. As one of the few Syrians in the community, I often felt that I was living a "double life." Within the confines of my home, I embraced the food, language and traditional clothing of my family's homeland. Yet when I left the house, I easily blended into the nuances of the American culture, which followed very different rules. At a young age, I learned how to juggle the subtleties of each culture and adapt the most important and beneficial aspects of each into my own personality and behavior. Most importantly, I learned to take pride in my heritage and to share it eagerly with others.

My interest in diversity compelled me to take a college-level course in Women's Anthropology at the University of Pennsylvania, which is a renowned institution with a diverse student body. Looking back, the class was an excellent opportunity for me to explore my role as a multicultural woman. One of my most memorable activities was marching in Washington D.C. in response to the Supreme Court's decision in favor of affirmative action in college admissions. Regardless of which side the students were on, we were energized by the process of joining together to defend the school's policy and reputation. Through this experience, I came to truly understand the benefits of being part of a diverse learning community in which our voices are respected and heard.

Marching in Washington completely changed my life. When I returned to Sproul, I realized that its small town environment no longer fit the person I hoped to become. As a result, I decided to pursue my college education at a place that celebrates diversity. After all, a critical part of education is having the right to express my views and assimilate those of others. By sharing our unique opinions and experiences in a supportive environment, we can better understand new ideas and learn how to apply them to our own lives. I am applying to Harvard University primarily because of its demonstrated commitment to a diverse curriculum and interdisciplinary thinking. I am eager to part of a talented and diverse group of people who share their collective resources both inside and outside the classroom. With such a broad foundation, I will be better prepared to achieve my long-term goal of promoting gender equality in Syria.

Our Assessment: This essay addresses several points in just three paragraphs, including the candidate's goals, commitment to activism, and multicultural background. Most importantly, it explains her desire to complete her education in a diverse environment that would allow her to continually expand her viewpoint.

Your Fit for a Particular School   (400 word limit)

After surviving the fiscal collapse in Brazil, I decided to study economics to prepare for a career at the IMF or World Bank. In 2009, I participated in the IMF Student Leadership Conference in Washington, DC, which included several lectures about the need for emergency funding in Africa, South America and the Middle East. Through these discussions – and my AP course in Economics - I acknowledged the need (and opportunity) for someone like me to work at the IMF as an advocate for change.

Dartmouth's exceptional program in economics is an ideal fit for my background and skills. With relevant courses in finance and management, I will be better prepared to meet the complex challenges of a global economy. Located near the financial districts in Boston and New York City, your program offers a unique opportunity for me to network among people who influence the world markets. Dartmouth's faculty members don't just teach mathematical models; they originate them. I am eager to participate in a community of international students who are committed to learning from each another. Beyond my coursework, I hope to form many long-lasting friendships and business relationships by participating in relevant clubs, internships, and outside activities.

Dartmouth is also the perfect place to hone my skill in oration, which will enhance my ability to lead a professional team. To overcome my shyness in a new country, I joined debate to build my self-confidence and to become more comfortable speaking English. Within a year, I became a seasoned public speaker who competed successfully in international competitions. Last summer, my team placed third out of 125 teams at UCLA's Debate Program. I was also one of 20 students who was accepted to Stanford University's selective "Oration Lab" program for advanced debaters. I regularly use my speaking skills to benefit others. Since tenth grade, I have worked as a volunteer English tutor at a non-profit daycare center in downtown Oakland. I plan to bring this same enthusiasm to Dartmouth's "Speakfest", which organizes debates in disadvantaged communities in New Hampshire. In addition, I plan to augment my own skills by joining Dartmouth's world renowned debate team.

To prepare for a career in international economics, I need to develop a solid background in languages, diplomacy, history and communications. I also need an educational environment with a focus on diversity and high achievement, where I can hone my debate skills and use them to help others. I need the unique resources and experiences that only Dartmouth can provide.

Our Assessment: This essay makes a logical link between the candidate's goals and the offerings at Dartmouth. It also reveals the many clubs and activities that she will contribute to, which will develop her as a person. As a result, the committee recognized the unique ways that she would enhance campus life.

Your Fit for a Particular School   (250 word limit)

Compared to other schools, the University of California at Davis offers the best opportunity for me to succeed in my chosen major and explore my passion for athletics. Last year, I was intrigued by the material in my AP Physics and Chemistry classes. After considerable research, I have decided to pursue a major in chemical engineering, which will allow me to further explore my interest in science and mathematics. UC-Davis offers the best undergraduate program in mechanical engineering in the state, including an excellent faculty and a broad range of classes. To me, these resources ensure that UC-Davis will provide the tools I will need to be successful in the field. As an added bonus, the program's excellent reputation will enhance my credibility when I apply for future jobs and graduate programs.

On a practical basis, UC-Davis also offers a familiar place for me to begin my college experience, without struggling to find my way around town or my place on campus. As an Oakland resident with a strong GPA, I am also eligible for in-state-tuition and a state merit scholarship, which will make UC-Davis the most affordable educational option. Finally, I am also interested in attending a university that will allow me to make athletics an important part of my life. After touring the UC-Davis athletic department, I am excited about the possibility of having access to such a well-equipped facility. For me, the goal of a college education is to prepare myself for the future in the most enjoyable, comfortable, and effective way. After considering the merits of several schools, I have concluded that UC-Davis is the best place for me to do that.

Our Assessment: In this essay, the candidate summarizes the many reasons that UC-Davis is the best fit for him, including cost and proximity. Although these factors were undoubtedly important to him, he wisely presented them in the second paragraph, rather than the first. By opening the essay with his discussion about science and engineering, the candidate showed the committee that his top priority was getting an excellent education. The financial aspects of UC-Davis were a secondary consideration.

Your Fit for a Particular School   (500 word limit)

From the statue of Daniel Webster to the sprawling Baker-Berry Library, Dartmouth College is a distinguished campus with impeccable standards and a rich source of history. To me, Dartmouth's founder, the Reverend Eleazar Wheelock, is the model of a true leader. Among his many accomplishments, Rev. Wheelock championed the development of a higher educational program that was based on a multidisciplinary model, noting that "Genius without education is like silver in the mine." Inspired by Rev. Wheelock, I have a keen appreciation for Dartmouth's goal of training students to learn, grow, and eventually give back to society. I would be honored to cultivate my talents among a dedicated group of like-minded peers.

Among the numerous majors that interest me, I am most attracted to global economics, which will allow me to use my analytical strengths in a socially relevant way. As part of my curriculum, I hope to take classes at Tuck School of Business, which offers a rigorous and flexible curriculum to suit the needs of a rapidly changing global business environment. In recent years, Dartmouth has done an enviable job of using the Internet to disseminate information via the HathiTrust Digital Library. I am fascinated by the multifaceted topics on China and India, including insightful comments from people across the globe. As a student at Dartmouth, I hope to contribute to the content in the digital library and enhance the learning experience of my fellow students.

Throughout my life, I have been fascinated by the impact of domestic economic policies upon a nation's wealth. I have also wondered how economists use various statistical tools to quantify changes in income and productivity. By specializing in global economics, I can also use my mathematical aptitude to quantify the ongoing changes in the world economy. Whenever possible, I have pursued relevant projects in this area. In my junior year, I conducted a research project to examine the collapse of the U.S. real estate market, due to the risky loans offered by domestic banks and mortgage companies. By using my knowledge of Economics and Statistics, I explained the inevitable impact of adjustable rate mortgages on unsuspecting buyers, who were unable to handle their escalating payments. My project, although exciting, revealed the rudimentary nature of my background in economics and statistics. By specializing in global economics, I will learn how and why the mortgage debacle occurred and identify viable ways to prevent a recurrence.

To confront the ongoing problems in our world economy, we need leaders who are bold, knowledgeable, and able to develop practical and innovative solutions. By pursuing my degree in economics at Dartmouth, including business classes at Tuck, I will learn how to create a positive relationship between the business world and the society that drives it. On a personal and professional basis, the future will hold no boundaries.

Our Assessment: From start to finish, this essay provides extraordinary details that reveal the author's passion for the school. She clearly understands the many ways that Dartmouth (and Tuck) will allow her to achieve her professional goals.

Chapter 6: A Topic of your Choice

The Common Application offers candidates the chance to choose their *own* topic for the essay, rather than answer a specific prompt. Additionally, several schools ask students if there is anything else they would like to submit as part of their application. Theoretically, students can answer this question any way they like. In reality, the *best* approach is to discuss a topic the committee would not hear about any other way. Ideally, the information you present should complement – rather than duplicate – the material in your other essays for that school.

The following essays vary widely in length and topic, but they all handled this question in an extraordinary way. By design, we have grouped the essays in the following sub-categories:

Childhood & Personality Development
Musical or Artistic Passion
Athletic Achievements Awards and Their Significance to You

For each essay, we have also indicated whether or not the essay was written for the Common Application or to answer a specific question for a college or university. (<u>Note</u>: If the essay was for a specific school, we have also indicated the specified length limit for the response.)

To protect the privacy of the writer, the names of all people, classes, schools, places, teams, activities, and companies have been changed.

Childhood Experiences   (500 word limit)

Three years ago, my sister Ling was diagnosed with multiple myeloma at age four. This horrific experience, which required her to undergo months of painful treatments, completely changed our family. During her chemotherapy, I was Ling's closest confidante and role model. Ironically, although I was a decade older than Ling, I came to admire her as much as she admired me. Her treatments were extremely painful, but Ling never cried or complained. In fact, her strength and courage radiated throughout our entire family.

Over time, the side effects from chemotherapy were difficult to watch. To avoid nausea, Ling had to take many drugs that left her feeling tired and drowsy. Eventually, her hair fell out in big clumps. To prevent Ling from feeling "different," my father and brother shaved their heads so that they would look alike. Later, when Ling was in isolation, my mother and I taught her how to play Fish. As expected, Ling laughed endlessly at these simple gestures to show our solidarity. Regardless of what the future held, we were determined to face this disease as a strong and loving family.

In subsequent years, I was amazed by the "Ling effect," which I gratefully called the unique combination of Ling's will to live and the compassionate care of her physicians. After several months of treatments, Ling beat her disease and has been cancer-free for three years. She is now a healthy and energetic seven-year-old can easily beat me in card games.

Caring for Ling during a difficult time – and witnessing the ability of the medical team to save her life – inspired my decision to become a physician. After her recovery, I began to volunteer at the Cherished Children Pediatric Clinic, where the doctors and their staff provided loving care to dozens of patients with different types of cancer. I am intrigued by the innovative breakthroughs that allow these doctors to save the lives of deserving children like Ling. Eventually, I hope to use my skills to achieve the same goal.

By exploring my interest in medicine, I have identified my ability to lead by example. I am particularly motivated to take a stand when I see people who are sad and isolated. Before Ling's illness, I struggled to balance both halves of my Vietnamese-American heritage. Sadly, I did not seem to really fit in anywhere. My friends at school considered me "Asian," while my family in Vietnam considered me "American." I began to wonder if there would ever be a place that would accept every part of me.

I found that acceptance in a medical environment, where my race and culture were less important than my desire to make a difference. By working hard, setting goals, and building relationships with people from different backgrounds and cultures, I have gained a greater appreciation of who I am and what I have to offer. In college, I am eager to use my skills as a leader to promote a spirit of inclusion on campus. By doing so, I hope to set an excellent example for other students who are struggling to find their way.

This candidate was deeply affected by her sister's illness, which has thankfully responded to treatment. By writing about the recovery process, which bonded this family together, the author gives us considerable insight into how it helped her to identity her long-term goals.

Childhood Experiences   (600 word limit)

When I was five years old, I decided to take apart my portable radio in order to find out whose voices were coming from inside it. I carefully took apart all 12 pieces, only to discover that I had silenced the nice men and women who lived there. Through my tears, I told my mother the terrible deed that I had committed. After a tender hug, a good laugh, and more than a few Oreos, I learned my first scientific lesson: always find out who (or what) is inside the box before you dismantle it.

Afterwards, I spent the rest of my childhood reminding myself of that lesson. From that first ill-fated attempt with the radio to my more recent efforts to fix my own transmission, I have gained a reputation as the "girl who runs with mechanics." Needless to say, this is not what my parents had in mind when they decorated my childhood bedroom with pink ballerinas.

I have always been an inquisitive child, especially where science and machinery are concerned. When I was in the second grade, my teacher warned my dad that I was smart, but a handful. I asked questions that she couldn't answer and completed the science projects before she could recite the instructions. My parents were instantly intrigued. They thought I only dismantled appliances at home.

Over the years, my entire family, including my athletic brother Ben, has grown to accept and nurture my constant desire to tinker. When I was 10 years old, my parents scraped together enough money to buy an expensive encyclopedia set. I was awestruck by the world that it opened up to me. Within two weeks, I learned how to fix our broken, four-slice toaster. Later, during the summer, I helped my dad and Ben re-build the engine of our 88' Dodge Colt. Although I was years away from driving it, I felt like a hero. It was also a true epiphany for me about my personal talents and interests.

While other kids, including Ben, were reading comic books, I stayed up late studying electricity and carbine engines. My personal heroes became Albert Einstein and Benjamin Franklin, who invented almost every appliance I took apart. I was determined to understand their achievements. Although it would be years before I truly understood the theory of relativity, I knew that I wanted to make a comparable contribution to science.

On a practical basis, I have gotten my chance at the last two Illinois State Science Fairs. My projects placed well both years, including my most recent study on the role of surfactants on engine efficiency. But I was most proud of my family's reaction at the fair. Although neither of my parents were scientists, they visited every booth and read every contest entry. When approached by other parents, they proudly told everyone that their athletic (and somewhat shy) tomboy had won first place. They never mentioned that I hadn't gotten around to putting the lawn mower back together yet. Or that I used a piece from Ben's motorcycle for my contest entry. I was more touched by their unconditional acceptance than by the scholarship prize.

My parents also support my application to Harvard, and promise to provide the tuition money to finance my educational dream. But the deal is conditional. I had to make some major concessions about my behavior once I get to Cambridge. No challenging the teachers, they insist, and no taking apart anyone else's appliances. I agreed that I would somehow restrain my scientific curiosity and try to blend in with the crowd. They never noticed that I had my fingers crossed behind my back when I made that promise.......

This candidate's resume was filled with honors and awards for her many scientific achievements. As a result, the committee already knew that she was smart, driven, and talented. This essay told the personal side of the candidate's life story in a funny and lighthearted way. After reading it, the committee felt like they actually *knew* her, which was a testament to her decision to have fun with the essay and simply tell a story.

Childhood Experiences   (600 word limit)

I always thought that she looked like the fairy godmother in Snow White. Despite her advancing age, my paternal grandmother still has a kind smile and a luxurious head of long, curly blonde hair. "Not important", she says, whenever someone compliments her appearance. "My looks are a gift from my parents. I'd rather you judge me by my own talents." Stubborn, hard-working and opinionated to a fault, my grandmother Beth has been one of the most positive influences in my life.

I can't remember a time when she didn't take me to work with her on Saturdays, to the ice cream shop she owned on Manhattan's Lower East Side, where there are still jukeboxes in the booths and real Coca-Cola flowing in the fountains. Long after her peers had retired to the sunny beaches of Florida, my grandmother Beth still runs her business 6 days a week. "Work is good for the soul", she insists, as she diligently scrubs the granite countertops. I marvel at her stamina. Despite being four times my age, she still runs circles around me.

My parents never told me much about Beth's life, except that it was a shame that she had it so hard. Apparently, she was a single parent at a young age, after losing my grandfather to cancer. The ice cream shop was Beth's only source of income and her only business "education." For nearly thirty years, she struggled to provide her children with a secure future. My parents feel badly that Beth never had the chance to complete her education. "What she could have accomplished," they muse, "if she had made something of her life."

Ironically, my experiences in the ice cream parlor have given me a different perspective. I think that Beth is the smartest and most successful person I know. She has a job that she loves doing, even at an advanced age. She has high work standards that she is not afraid to impose on her employees. Beth treats her helpers well, but she expects them to work hard and treat the customers right. And she never complains, no matter how long or hard her day has been. Beth knows the name of every man, woman and child in her neighborhood and is a loyal friend to them. At the shop, she is committed to giving every customer a pleasurable experience and a quality product..... and she has instilled every one of those values in me.

Beth is excited that I am applying to college and hopes that I get accepted at a good school. She looks forward to hearing about my experiences and what I will learn from the best minds that the Ivy League has to offer. But I am convinced that my college education will truly be a two-way street. Princeton will provide me with an exceptional education, but I have something to offer you, too.

I have learned valuable lessons about life, about the value of hard work, and the importance of handling grief and setbacks. I have also learned how to smile and do a good job even when I would rather be home relaxing. I have also learned how to run a business and develop loyal customers. And I have learned that it's not the external appearance of someone that is important, but the values they hold inside. I will share those lessons with everyone I meet at Princeton and later in my career.

And I will be honest about where I obtained such a well-rounded life experience. Not only at Princeton, but from the time I was born, at the knees of the wisest, most charitable woman I know. I have received a wonderful education every Saturday afternoon, cleaning floors and growing close to my beautiful, golden-haired grandmother Beth.

Our Assessment: This author used the same essay to answer a question about her most influential role model. Although it is simply written, it is honest, heartfelt, and extremely moving. It also showed the committee a side of the applicant they would not have learned about any other way.

Childhood Experiences   (Common Application: 750 word limit)

Long before I was born, my parents wrestled with the decision about where they would live. My mother, a mid-western farm girl, desperately hoped that my dad could find a surgical residency in a rural area. Unfortunately, the only rotation in his specialty was in Los Angeles, where my mom reluctantly moved. According to legend, you could hear her kicking and screaming from miles away.

Although I enjoyed growing up in the land of beaches, Hollywood, and perpetual sunshine, my mom always wanted more for me. She worried that my cultural background would be limited if I did not experience my rural heritage. Thus, she decided when I was 13 that I should spend the summer with my grandparents in rural Iowa. If given the choice, I would have preferred to get a root canal without novocaine.

Don't get me wrong: it's not that I didn't love Grandmo and PaPa. They called and wrote often and always sent me great Christmas gifts. But the thought of actually living in the country for the summer was as appealing to me as swimming in a sweater. Since I had little leverage at 13, my mom's desire for my cultural development won out. Off I went to Ottumwa, kicking and screaming as hard as my mom could imagine.

I didn't realize at the time what a memorable experience the trip would be. I had been raised in a large metropolitan area where the pace was fast and frenetic. As successful professionals, my parents equipped our home with every luxury that money could buy, including three cars, a widescreen TV, and multiple cell phones. For entertainment, we had more than three hundred cable channels and dozens of first-run movie theatres. In Los Angeles, you could be in a coma and never be bored.

In contrast, Ottumwa had a grocery store and a post office. All of the telephones were rotary and there wasn't even basic cable service. But the worst part was that my grandparents didn't even see that it was a problem. They welcomed me for the summer with open arms, telling me repeatedly that I would have the time of my life. I was convinced there was something funny in the water.

But a strange thing happened during those long, hot, musty weeks in 2006. I started to make the best of boring Ottumwa. Every day, I accompanied Grandmo on her morning chores and to her afternoon volunteer work at the local veterinary clinic. I helped her to run errands and to cook and clean the huge house that she shared with PaPa. And in the evenings, I sat around the dinner table and listened to their familiar stories about buying the farm when they first got married and the years they scrimped and sacrificed to make it a profitable business. I also learned about my mother's passion for riding and grooming horses, which had begun on that very farm. After mounting a horse for the first time that summer, I realized why my mother loved it so much.

Late one night, Grandmo took out an old, yellowed photo album from the attic and slowly went through it with me. She had a sweet story about every photo, most of which brought a glint of laughter to her eyes. Nearly every story taught me more about my mom's hopes and dreams for the future. I saw pictures of her milking cows, competing in state fairs and delivering puppies. By age fourteen, she even drove a tractor!

For the first time, I realized how out of place my mother felt in LA, where she was surrounded by glass and concrete buildings that were less than 10 years old. In this crime ridden city, we have unlimited money and recreation, but we don't have peace and quiet. Instead, we protect our wealth with a state-of-the-art security system that contributes to our self-imposed isolation. As the summer wore on, I began to appreciate the quietness in Iowa, the smell of fresh air, and the comfort of life-long friendships.

I would love to say that I returned to LA a changed person who never drank a slurpee or watched HBO ever again. But that wouldn't be true. I appreciated being back in my familiar environment, but I returned with a broader perspective of what I considered to be "home." Since then, I have spent every summer in Iowa, and my parents try to accompany me for at least part of the trip. It's a restorative experience for everyone. Although I will probably never milk a cow with the same skill as my mom, I am proud to include it on my list of life experiences. I am also privileged to have Grandmo and PaPa in my life, who might not know what a DVD player is, but are otherwise the "hippest" people I know. They were right about my first summer there being memorable. Sometimes, the places you are dragged to kicking and screaming offer you the most important life lessons.

Our Assessment: This essay, although casually written, is filled with humor and charm. It also gives the reader considerable insight into the candidate's personality.

Childhood Experiences   (600 word limit)

I clearly remember the smell of her hair on hot California nights. My mother would take a reprieve from her role as a caregiver and relax in a jasmine-scented tub, surrounded by the classical notes of Bach and the glow from dozens of small scented candles. Later, she would emerge from her bath with a warm smile, renewed patience, and a sense of serenity that I envied, even in my childhood innocence.

As an only child, I enjoyed a close relationship with my mother, who had high expectations for me in school, music, and gymnastics. I always suspected that she was seeking to fulfill her own dreams through me, having deferred her own professional goals to marry my father and become a doctor's wife. My mother never complained, but I occasionally sensed her disappointment when I failed to pursue an opportunity that she felt was right for me. In my heart, I knew that I was the second chance at life that my mother never had.

During my teenage years, we had great conversations about dicey subjects such as politics, dating, school problems and friends. To my continual amazement, my mother was right about more things than I would ever admit. We had a frustrating battle about clothes. My mom hated my "grunge" look of low-riding pants, clunky boots and ill-fitting tee shirts. She never missed a chance to drag me to the mall and get me to try on pleated skirts and sweater sets. When I modeled these outfits, I was startled by my reflection in the dressing room mirror; I looked like a smaller, younger version of my mother, who was ready to set the world on fire as a future executive. Although the clothes didn't suit me, I often wished that I had her confidence and dedication.

I never imagined that she would be gone now, lost to me at a time when I need her guidance the most. As I apply to college, I wish I could get savvy advice from her about applying to her alma mater. I never realized that cancer could strike so quickly and claim someone so strong and determined within a few months.

My mother is the one person I couldn't imagine living without, yet now I have to. I have survived two Christmases without her, yet I still feel her presence when I select gifts and decorate the tree. It's hard to describe my mother's energy, which is still so powerful and comforting. Whenever I am having a hard day or facing a tough decision, I sometimes "hear" her words, which help me to find the best solution. I know that in some way she is still guiding my life and cheering me on from the sidelines.

My mother would be proud to know that I am applying to Princeton, which is her alma mater. While I cannot promise that I will grace the campus wearing the tailored suits and sweater sets that my mom would have selected, I will bring her wisdom, guidance, and spirit to all of my endeavors.

I am in every way my mother's legacy. As such, I am determined to make her proud of me. In the next four years, I will make the most of every academic opportunity that comes my way and reach for every dream I have. Like my mom, I will take great joy in the amazing people, places, and activities that a university such as Princeton will afford. And when the going gets tough, really tough, I will relax my mind by taking a warm, jasmine-scented bath by candlelight. In those quiet moments, I know in my heart that I can accomplish anything.

Our Assessment: Many candidates write about the loss of a loved one, but few achieve the proper balance between hope and sadness. This essay does the best job we have ever seen. By discussing her mother's impact on her life, the candidate gives us a personal glimpse into the person she really is. In the final paragraphs, we also share the pain of her loss.

Artistic or Musical Talent   **(Common Application: 750 word limit)**

Last winter, I prepared my application for a prestigious summer arts program that I was extremely eager to attend. After passing the state level, I reviewed my portfolio with my art teacher, who assured me that I had an excellent chance of being accepted into this highly competitive program. Consequently, when I received a letter informing me that I had been placed on the waiting list for the Rhode Island School of Design Visual Arts Program, the world literally came to a halt. Before that moment, I had defined myself primarily by my artistic passion and skill. My rejection from this program, which felt like a mortal blow, forced me to reevaluate my identity - and future - as an artist.

The following month, I researched the life of Eugene Delacroix for a class assignment. I was stunned to discover that this distinguished artist, who was one of the Old Masters, had been rejected from some of the top art academies in France. In an instant, I felt a personal connection to this man, who refused to let short-term setbacks derail his long-term aspirations. I also acknowledged my own tendency to let my fear of rejection hold me back. For something as subjective as art, it is impossible to please everyone. The key is being strong enough to handle a bad review. If Eugene Delacroix had the confidence to bounce back from a disappointment, I could certainly do the same.

Afterwards, I began to research and analyze some of Delacroix's lesser-known etchings, which helped me to refine my own sense of purpose as an artist. Like me, Delacroix loved to investigate the political, social, and ethical aspects of his world. During times of turmoil, such as the Spanish Inquisition and Napoleon's invasion of Spain, Delacroix depicted the darkness of these atrocities in his work. At first, the explicit images were difficult for me to view, because I had never witnessed violence in my own life. At the same time, I admired Delacroix's courage in depicting historical events that were not aesthetically pleasing.

Ultimately, Delacroix's paintings opened my mind to what I could accomplish as an artist. Beforehand, I tended to avoid any type of risk. I certainly did not have the confidence to explore controversial topics that expose the worst aspects of humanity. Afterwards, in my AP Art course, I challenged myself by delving further into the meaning of every piece in my portfolio. Rather than focus on the grade I would receive, I took the time to create unique pieces that expressed my thoughts on issues that were significant to me, such as societal oppression throughout history. Specifically, I created my own interpretation of Delacroix's *Greece Expiring on the Ruins of Messolonghi*, which connected my personal struggles to those of the women in Greece. On a practical basis, this approach was risky, because it limited the number of pieces I could produce. Yet, on an artistic and intellectual basis, it was significantly more rigorous and satisfying.

Every piece required me to merge divergent political and cultural concepts in a creative and personal way. They also required a meticulous level of detail that my previous pieces did not. Ultimately, by challenging myself in this manner – and by following Delacroix's example – I created a provocative portfolio that earned the highest possible score. Most importantly, I developed the confidence I needed to view the world with a different lens and push the limits of my creativity as an artist.

Ironically, I might never have taken this risk – or embarked on this emotional and professional journey – if I had been accepted into the summer program at Rhode Island School of Design. This setback, which initially seemed like the end of the world, was the catalyst I needed to mature as an artist. As I continue to explore my talent in college, I will embrace every experience, whether positive or negative, as the opportunity that it is – a chance to learn more about myself, my art, and the impact I can have on the world around me.

<u>Our Assessment</u>: This candidate used the same essay to answer a question about a challenge she had overcome to achieve her goals. By choosing a difficult subject (being waitlisted for a program that she really wanted to attend), she took the reader of a journey that transformed her sadness into maturity and self-awareness. The essay was well-perceived.

Artistic or Musical Talent   **(500 word limit)**

After several years of "enrichment overdose," my parents decided to limit my extracurricular activities to just two or three of my favorite pursuits. When they asked me to choose my activities, they were nearly floored by my decision. Rather than sweat on the softball field or kick my way through karate class, I chose the relative tranquility of viola lessons.

Ironically, my appreciation for the viola was neither intense nor automatic. Between the ages of six and ten, I hated my Thursday night lessons. Every week, I rushed home from school to cram in my half-hearted practice, followed by a two-hour lesson and exhausting ride home. At the time, I silently cursed Mrs. Hancock, who made me repeat the same difficult chords over and over again. On my worst days, I questioned whether I would ever get a song right. Yet, when I re-examine my childhood, I can truthfully say that mastering the viola became the most rewarding part of my life.

My victories were small and subtle, as I gradually mastered my instrument. Each new step caused a dramatic leap in my self-esteem, as Mrs. Hancock jovially celebrated my skill. Now, I view the viola as a rare oasis in my otherwise insane schedule. What better way to relax in the middle of a chaotic day? Thanks to my viola, I can bomb a trig test, and be in heaven ten minutes later. Completely relaxed, I rock back and forth to the soothing rhythm, as my arms work in harmony to create a vibrating melody. With my eyes closed, I marvel at my ability to make time stand still, as I become immersed in the wonderful world of music.

Although I have played other instruments, including the cello and the piano, the viola will always be my favorite. Whether blustering or sweet, the viola offers deep tones and a surprisingly broad range of expression. As I perfect my skills, I have become enamored by the creative portion of making music, as exemplified by masters like Tosca Kramer, Lillian Fuchs and Johann Sebastian Bach. Regardless of my mood, their brilliant music can make me forget the problems of my day and lose myself in the ebullience of the piece. Whether I listen to the viola or play it myself, I can rejoice in the beauty that the elegant instrument represents.

Yet, sadly, I must do so without the company of my beloved teacher. Three days before my sixteenth birthday, Mrs. Hancock died unexpectedly, without knowing the influence she had on my life. More than anything, I wish that she could hear me play the viola in my school band, which is where I feel most alive. Whenever I asked for direction on a particularly complicated piece, her advice was always the same. "Play from the heart." Thanks to her, I always do.

Artistic or Musical Talent   (500 word limit)

The tools of my first business venture were quite simple: hair curlers, a few nail files, a detailed price list, and of course, my faithful calculator. To satisfy my advertising needs, I also made a big sign with silver glitter that read "Lucy's Coiffure." At age seven, my desire to make a few dollars to buy new toys inspired me to set up a beauty parlor in my family's apartment. As I watched my mom undergo her daily beauty ritual, I realized that there was a market for similar services in my own my family. My parents and older sister were pleasantly surprised that I would think of such an idea, but they were not terribly encouraging. Despite my lack of experience, I was determined to earn my own pocket money from my glamorous business.

Unfortunately, because of my young age, I was not allowed to let any strangers into our apartment. This restriction limited my potential client base to my friends and relatives, which was the death knell to a venture that thrived on volume. Without the ability to market the business, I eventually closed the shop and took down my sign. Yet, even today, I do not view the experience as a failure. My early days as a home-educated "beautician" were excellent preparation for my work as a makeup artist for our school's drama club, the Warren High School Players.

Since freshman year, I have worked on the makeup team for all eight productions, including the particularly challenging *Lion King*. Fortunately, from my early experience in cosmetology, I easily grasped the basics of applying stage makeup, including the use of wigs and prosthetics. The *Lion King*, however, presented special challenges. To learn how to apply the theatrical makeup for the animal characters, I attended a two-day workshop in New York City that was taught by renowned makeup artist Shirley Carter.   With Ms. Carter's help, I learned how to transform our teenage lead into a "wild beast" of Simba's magnitude. By the final performance, I had reduced my application time to less than two hours, which rivals that of professional makeup artists.

Although my childhood coiffure shop did not succeed, it was my first attempt to make a living in a creative venture. Eventually, I hope to use the same skills to become a professional makeup artist who transforms ordinary people into cinematic wonders. Through my work with the Warren High School Players, I have taken a giant step toward the fulfillment of this goal. Who knows? With a leap of faith and a healthy dose of luck, I may join the ranks of experts such as Shirley Carter, who have transformed their passion into a lucrative and enjoyable career.

Artistic or Musical Talent   (400 word limit)

Struck with panic, I hastily flipped through my music. As my heart pounded, I wondered what I was doing at the Chicago Convention Hall. Sure, I was a good violinist, but did I really have a chance to make the National High School Orchestra? What if I completely bombed? Or dropped my bow? Could I ever show my face again at St. Phillips Academy?

Fortunately, the tight audition schedule left me little time to think. I only had twenty minutes until my audition, which gave me just enough time to run through the entire passage. When my name was called, I tried to stifle the butterflies in my stomach. As my hands sweated and my mind tried to focus, I silently prayed that I wouldn't make a complete fool of myself.

That's the beauty of being a musician. The stage fright that paralyzed me for that split second, complete with butterflies in my stomach, empowered me to deliver one of the best performances of my career. I felt giddy when left the audition room; although my anxiety had waned, the adrenaline still rushed through my body for several minutes. A few hours later, when the results were posted, I experienced the same nervous fluttering in my stomach. I was delighted to place third in such a competitive pool of musicians.

The convention was a wonderful experience, both for the training I received and for the opportunity to make friends with other talented students. As we adapted to the group's sound, we began to play without reserve, which made our rehearsals seem like magic. While we played, I often gazed around the room and admired the skill of my peers, who had worked as long and hard as I did to win a place in the competition. Amidst such formidable talent, we blossomed under the conductor's tutelage and developed our techniques to their fullest.

Each time the orchestra played, we enjoyed a rare and powerful synergy, which fused the talent of each musician into a heavenly sound. I was honored beyond belief to be part of such a miracle. By the end of the week, we had transformed from a group of strangers into a cohesive team with an unbreakable bond. For a dedicated player like me, that is the glory of music.

Our Assessment: The opening of this essay is particularly strong. From the first line, it pulls the reader into the story and lets us feel the candidate's anxiety. Later, the essay eloquently explains the joy that he gets from being part of the orchestra. By sharing this story with the committee, the candidate showed a part of himself that would otherwise have been buried on his activity list.

Artistic or Musical Talent   (300 word limit)

Since early childhood, I have expressed my creativity through the visual arts. In junior high school, I explored my love of black and white photography by taking weekend classes at the Dade County Art Institute. Starting from scratch, I learned how to master my camera as the miraculous tool that it is. By adjusting a few settings and properly coordinating my subject and light source, I spent the summer of 2007 capturing on film the most wondrous moments of nature. For my work in this medium, I received the first place award in the 2008 Dade County Art Show and had my photographs published in *Miami Monthly* magazine.

In the summer of 2008, I decided to master glass etching, which required the use of intimidating power tools. Moving past my initial trepidation, I learned how to etch the glass by sandblasting, which gave my work a unique sense of balance and texture. Moreover, by arranging several glass panes into a sculpture, I moved my study into three dimensions; my resulting piece, which I named "*Tropical Oasis*," won first place in the 2009 Dade County Art Show.

Currently, I am working on canvas, using oil and acrylic in a Gouache style, which is also based on lines and balance. The most exciting aspect of painting is the use of color, which adds several dimensions to my creative spectrum. For any given painting, a tiny adjustment in a tint or shade can make the difference between boldness or subtlety, garishness or simplicity. Eventually, in my college studio work, I hope to augment my skills in these media with those in sculpture to create my own unique style of artistic expression.

Our Assessment: Although short, this essay summarizes the candidate's accomplishes as an artist in a detailed and creative way. It also indicates her intention to perfect her skills at the distinguished art programs to which she applied.

Artistic or Musical Talent   (400 word limit)

My greatest accomplishment is music, which is also my greatest passion. I started playing the violin and piano at age five and was "discovered" by a talent agent at age eight. Throughout my childhood, I competed rigorously in all types of events, including categories beyond my age group. Amazingly, although I competed against older musicians from around the world, I usually won the events.

Although I am justifiably proud of my achievements, I despise the labels "child prodigy" and "musical genius," which ignore the importance of discipline and skill in attaining my goals. For most of my life, I have trained for at least six hours per day after school, with no guarantee of competitive success. Fortunately, my efforts have paid off handsomely. I represented Korea in the 2008 Korean-American Friendship Holiday Concert, and later toured with the same group throughout Europe. In 2009, I won an original composition scholarship to the Royal Conservatory in London, which allowed me to train with Pamela Frank, who is a distinguished music composer from my native Seoul. Under her tutelage, I performed my own composition with the London Pops Orchestra on its tour of Rome, Madrid, and Vienna.

My long journey to musical success has thoroughly changed my character and self-awareness. Many years ago, my dad told me that "to succeed in this world is to fail deeply first." Indeed, I failed many times before I tasted success. Through these setbacks, I learned to set expectations well above my goal and to always aim higher than the norm. By pursuing my true passion, I also discovered that the process and the journey are more rewarding than the outcome.

My achievements in music gave me confidence in my ability to succeed in all areas of life. At a young age, I saw the phenomenal results of sacrifice, perseverance and having faith in myself. By competing – and winning – in a variety of locations and venues, I became confident of my ability to overcome disappointments and setbacks. I also learned to emulate and respect people whose talents are different from my own. Most importantly, my experiences as a musician have also taught me to define success in non-monetary terms. Long after the audience leaves the concert hall, music gives me a sense of satisfaction and fulfillment that money cannot buy.

Our Assessment: This essay focuses exclusively on what music *means* to the candidate and the unique life lessons it has taught her. Through it, the reader learns why the author is as tenacious and disciplined as she is. She also takes great pride in her accomplishments, which came from years of dedication and practice.

Artistic or Musical Talent   (400 word limit)

"Do, re, mi, fa, so, la, ti, do…"

A relative novice, I started to play my first musical instrument, an alto saxophone, during my sophomore year of high school. Dr. Morrow, our band coordinator, ran a tight ship. Even during exam week, she refused to shorten our mandatory three-hour daily practices. "Band is important, Carly. You can't excel without practice…" I was touched by her faith in me as a musician, and I learned to better coordinate my multiple responsibilities. When I completed my first performance, our Christmas concert, I was honored to be part of such a talented and professional group.

Our performance won first place in the statewide 2008 Christmas band competition. Every moment of the night was magical. With my music in front of me and my Selmer gold-lacquered saxophone around my neck, I waited for the signal to start. "1-2-3-4, 2-2-3-4, 3-2-3-4…" After five rests, I began my part in "Serendipity 2008," completely oblivious to the audience. Lost in the music, I was no longer nervous about being observed. I drifted into a personal fantasy that was inspired by the beautiful melodies we composed. After five minutes, I moved on to my second piece, "Falsetto Moss"…

Some say that I am destined to play an instrument because musical aptitude correlates strongly with my skills in the sciences and foreign languages. Although flattering, this theory neglects the tremendous commitment of time and energy that I have invested to become a talented musician. Over the years, I worked diligently to learn how to read music and improve my hand/eye coordination. I also developed the discipline to repeat the same piece over and over again, regardless of my level of frustration. Eventually, I came to appreciate the synergy of the band, in which the collective energy of our group raised the caliber of our own individual efforts.

I also fell in love with my sax for its therapeutic effect. Whenever I am stressed out, I get immediate relief by playing it. Perhaps this is what inspires the world's great musicians: their ability to use their talent to improve a listener's mood, to invoke a precious memory, or to produce an invigorating dance beat. As a budding musician, I share that magic and yearn to explore its power. Wherever my future leads me, I will explore my love of music by joining the Yale band, an all-girls jazz group, or maybe a large orchestra. Thanks to the inspiration of Dr. Morrow, I am determined to follow my muse and enjoy its myriad benefits.

Our Assessment: This essay repeats some of the same themes in the previous one: the importance of discipline, the willingness to practice long hours each day, and the joy of being part of a talented orchestra that encourages the pursuit of excellence. For aspiring musicians, these are the most common themes that the committee expects to see, which reflect the invaluable life lessons that music has instilled in them.

Athletic Achievement   (500 word limit)

His name was Chang. Although there were other competitors at the tournament, no one else posed any serious threat to my title. Throughout the five years that I had competed in the National Kickboxing

Tournament, I had easily won the black belt championship in my division. Chang, however, was the most phenomenal martial artist I had ever seen. His recent addition to my division made it a whole new game.

To be honest, my first assessment of my adversary left me queasy. Although Chang was identical to me in age and weight, he surpassed me in almost every aspect of our training. His feet were lightning fast and his hands were virtually invisible in their swiftness. Despite his small size, he had the power of a bear. As I watched Chang from the sidelines, I noticed that his form and techniques were nearly perfect, but I refused to psyche myself out. Although I had never beaten anyone even remotely as extraordinary, victory was not impossible. After all, I was the state champion.

As I quietly evaluated Chang's strengths, I also discovered my best hope for beating this incredible foe. Despite his obvious gifts, Chang had a major weakness: he was lazy. He didn't practice long enough. He worked hard, but not as hard as I did. Basking in overconfidence, he didn't think that he had to. Mistake! Knowing the power of my own tenacity, I knew that I had found my passage to triumph.

In my own martial arts career, my success has hinged almost entirely on my perseverance. What I lacked in initial skill and form, I more than made up for in relentless practice. After winning a few regional titles, I still retained a fighting spirit and maintained a rigorous training schedule. Every evening, I kicked, blocked, and punched at an imaginary opponent in my room. Over time, the hundreds of hour of constant drilling had improved my techniques and speed to the point where my skills were instinctive. I was ready for a challenge like Chang.

On the day of the championship match, Chang looked as confident as ever. Adrenaline raced through my body as I stepped into the ring. We bowed to each other - and to the instructor - and the match began. For the longest time, we were evenly matched; his strength against my endurance made us the most unlikely of competitors. The score was tied when time ran out, which forced us to go into sudden death. Whoever scored the next point would win.

I was tired beyond belief. The grueling two points I had already won had nearly sapped my stamina. Somehow, I needed to score another point to enjoy a taste of victory. Although Chang seemed unfazed, I refused to allow him to discourage me. I focused my entire being, my entire consciousness, on overcoming my nemesis. All of my training, every cell in my body, and every drop of desire was directed to that single purpose as I exploded through his defenses and drove a solitary fist to its mark.

Sweet, sweet victory! Through sweaty determination, I somehow accomplished the impossible. I beat Chang, I retained my title, and discovered that perseverance really does deliver its own just rewards. As a competitor, this one experience, this single moment, changed me forever. For a split second, I was the best.

Our Assessment: This essay literally takes the reader into the ring as the candidate wins his championship match. It is short, focused, and masterfully written.

Athletic Achievement   (400 word limit)

Playing varsity football has changed my entire outlook on life. Before my freshman year, I was a shy person with impossibly low self-esteem. Even the simplest challenges, like making new friends, seemed difficult to accomplish. Football changed all of that.

On the first day of freshman practice, the team warmed up with a game of touch football. In such a talented group of players, I was extremely intimidated. While others jockeyed for position, hoping to be thrown the ball, I was petrified of making a mistake and ruining a play. I was equally quiet in the classroom, where I refrained from asking questions, afraid that they might be considered too stupid by my classmates. All the while, I came home each night physically and mentally exhausted.

As time passed, I continued to fear making mistakes and getting blamed by my screaming coaches and angry teammates, yet I stayed on the team and occasionally got to play. Eventually, of course, my greatest fears came true. During my sophomore season, I botched several plays as a backup guard, which fortunately did not change the outcome of the game. The first time the coach chewed me out, I thought I was going to die.....but I didn't. In fact, I received empathetic grins from my teammates who had been in similar situations. Eventually, I came to realize that part of the game was making mistakes; the only "perfect" players were the ones I saw on television and in the movies. As a varsity player on the Bristol High School football team, I proceeded to earn my fair share of both accolades and criticism. Learning to accept the feedback, whether justified or not, made me a changed man.

Over the years, playing football has taught me what it takes to succeed. From months of tough practices, I have gained a solid work ethic. From my coaches and teammates, I have learned how to cooperate with others to achieve a common goal. But most importantly, I have gained self-confidence in all aspects of my life. If I fail, it doesn't matter if the crowd mocks or ridicules me; I'll just try again. As my coach often says, "You must risk failure in order to gain success." With a positive mindset, I have discovered that nothing is impossible; in fact, the bravest players actually welcome the challenge. Playing football has taught me that it is irrelevant if I succeed or fail; it is only important that I continue to test myself and discover the limits of my potential.

Our Assessment: This essay, although ostensibly about athletics, is actually about the impact of football on the candidate's life. By making mistakes on the field (and making peace with them), he gained the confidence he needed to build solid friendships and succeed in the classroom. Without taking those risks, the candidate would never have accomplished so much in his high school career.

Athletic Achievement   (300 word limit)

Over the past four years, I have trekked the entire length of the Appalachian Trail, cycled 300 miles across Pennsylvania, and rock climbed in northern Montana. Yet the most rewarding activities are those in which I have combined my passion for sports with my commitment to charity work. Recently, I served as the cyclist escort in the IBM Marathon for Elisa Evans, who is an activist for the rights of the handicapped. Over 300 cyclists participated in the marathon, which raised over $182,000 for the cause. Last month, I served as the volunteer coordinator for Cycle Aide activities in Pennsylvania, including a clothing drive and a 90-mile Prediction Ride to benefit the tsunami victims in Sri Lanka.

My commitment to athletics is particularly impressive considering the dismal state of my health as a child. To the amazement of people who meet me today, I started high school as a chubby girl who had never participated in sports. Nearly 40 lbs overweight, I had trouble walking around the block without losing my breath. Thanks to the support of Audrey Bowers, our high school track coach, I decided that good health was not only possible, but essential. By committing myself to a formal fitness program, I lost weight, improved my health, and became a vocal advocate for the lifelong benefits of exercise. Ms. Bowers literally saved my life.

From my participation in athletics, I have developed several important life skills. First, through years of hard work and continuous training, I have a strong sense of discipline, which has enhanced my character, work ethic, and perseverance. Through my charity work, I have learned how to lead by example and to put the needs of others before my own. Above all, sports have increased my love of life. Through hiking, rock climbing, and cycling, I have experienced pain, sacrifice, adversity, and success. My exposure to these feelings, which embody the entire essence of being, has enabled me to truly appreciate my life.

Our Assessment: The appeal of this essay is similar to that of the previous one – it explains how athletics have made the candidate a healthier, happier, and more successful person. As an added bonus, this essay documents the author's charity work, which was the subject of her primary essay. Her dramatic weight loss (and amazing personal transformation) deeply impressed the admissions committee.

Athletic Achievement   (300 word limit)

In addition to my academic interests, I have always been passionate about playing rugby. I competed on my junior high school's varsity team, which placed first in the Connecticut state tournament when I was in the eighth grade. Unlike my academic pursuits, which tended to be solitary, rugby taught me how to be a team player, as our success depended on our mutual cooperation and gamesmanship. In addition to mastering our individual skills, we challenged each other on the field, which raised the level of our game. Further, through my role as Team Captain, I developed the necessary leadership skills to maintain the team's cohesiveness.

I continued my pursuit of rugby at Exeter Academy, where I was a starting member of the campus varsity team. For three consecutive years, we placed first in several national rugby tournaments. In my senior year, we were invited to train for the United States' first entry into the Olympic rugby competition. I was honored by the opportunity to practice with some of the best names in the sport, including Gareth Edwards and Jason

Little. With their generous coaching and assistance, I miraculously earned a spot on the United States Olympic Team. To everyone's amazement, we captured the Bronze Medal while representing the nation in Seoul.

It is not an exaggeration to say that rugby has changed my life. After the Olympics, I began to coach a junior high school rugby team in Bridgeport. In addition to improving my physical fitness, coaching enhances my sense of optimism and gives me a positive way to interact with children. By working with future rugby stars, I have a coveted chance to give other talented players the same enthusiasm, dedication and support that my childhood coaches gave me.

Our Assessment: Although this candidate won an Olympic medal for playing rugby, he did not write about that experience in his primary application essay (which discussed his desire to become a physician). Instead, he presented the material in this short answer essay for his school of choice, which eagerly accepted him.

Significant Awards or Honors   (600 word limit)

As the clock started to tick, the frantic countdown began. Pencils scribbled. Brains clashed. Perspiration surfaced, which challenged even the strongest brand of deodorant. As I searched for a solution to a problem, I was incredibly tenacious. *Think, Amber. Think.*

With one minute left, I was stuck. *Arghh...... How do I factor these polynomials?* Time was running out, with no miracle in sight. With 30 seconds left, I finally recalled how to solve the last problem, but the clock was against me. "Pencils down! Time for team set!"

OK, no problem. Don't panic. I didn't finish, but we'll make up for it in the next round. As I gazed into the eyes of my fatigued squad, I was determined to motivate the troops. "Let's go! We're in World War III with these other teams - let's solve these problems..." No answer. No reaction. Although I resisted my urge to sigh, I knew I would have to fight the battle alone...... again. Fortunately, I was up to the challenge.

I gave it every drop of energy I had, using brain cells I didn't know existed. Although the problems were stunningly complex, I was determined to win. Yet after five excruciating minutes, a voice announced: "Kennedy High is in second place with 129 points..." *Arghh...it hurts. Second place again.*

No, this wasn't a military exercise or even rocket science. This was a grueling match between eight Mathletes teams in Southern California. A haven for Type-A math enthusiasts, Mathlete competitions pit the most talented students from each school against each other in a highly pressured battle of wits. As the captain of my squad, I was determined to win. No polynomial was too complicated, no trigonometry concept too vague, no word problem too convoluted. I was the woman to beat.

Whatever the final score in any match, I always gave it my best shot - a truly herculean effort. Yet, in Mathletes, my individual performance was irrelevant, because the scores and rankings are tabulated for the whole team, not for a single member. In this particular match, my individual points couldn't compensate for the ones that were lost by the rest of the squad.

Several teachers wonder why I enjoy Mathletes so much because the stress is overwhelming. Although we have won first place at three regional competitions, a trophy at the national level continues to elude us. Fortunately, I am motivated by the intrinsic rewards of these events, rather than any type of external validation. In addition to challenging my mind and igniting my competitive spirit, Mathletes also gave me a confident personality.

After a difficult adjustment to my new high school, I "found myself" when I joined Mathletes. As the captain of the squad, I developed self-confidence, leadership skills, and the ability to nurture others. More importantly, Mathletes taught me how to endure the greatest failures with poise and dignity. Some call it character, others call it class, while others call it grace under pressure. Thanks to Mathletes, I have "it" in spades.

By surviving failure with panache, I have become immune to the risk-aversion and paralysis that prevent people from testing the limits of their potential. I tackle challenges that others would never consider, and I take pride in our efforts, whether we win or lose. Even if we never win first place, we are already winners in ways that I never understood before I became a Mathlete.

Significant Awards or Honors   (500 word limit)

The moment the telephone rang, I knew that something was wrong. Throughout the evening, I had a vague premonition that someone needed my help. Before he learned how to drive, my good friend Joshua made the mistake of piling five of my closest friends into his father's car for a "quick spin." As expected, the combination of darkness, ice, and underage drinking led to a terrible disaster.

When I reached the accident site, I was thankful to see all of my friends alive and well, but distraught from the experience. Fortunately, the police officer did not suspect alcohol abuse, so Joshua did not have to take a breathalyzer test. Sp, technically, my friends got off "scot-free." Yet a remark from the mechanic quickly snapped us back to reality. "You kids are very lucky; most cars destroyed this badly contain corpses, rather than survivors." In the prolonged silence that followed, we acknowledged the significance of the accident: my friends had cheated death that night.

Throughout the rest of the evening, we discussed how vulnerable we suddenly felt. No one is invincible, including my good friends. In a split second, Joshua made a single bad decision with potentially irreversible consequences. Despite my initial fears, I kept my composure and offered my friends the support that they deserved. I didn't share my personal thoughts about the true cause of the accident, which was drunk driving.

Joshua's near-miss made a profound impact on me and reinforced my commitment to Students Against Drunk Driving (SADD). Although I was already a member of the group, my participation had been limited to attending an occasional meeting. I never volunteered to be a designated driver and I had certainly never taken anyone's keys away from them. That all changed with Joshua's accident. After nearly losing a car full of friends, I was determined to do everything possible to prevent another senseless accident due to underage drinking.

In 2009, I was elected President of Warren High School's first chapter of SADD. My first directive was to implement a zero tolerance policy for alcohol at our Junior and Senior Proms. At both events, I arranged for designated drivers for anyone who was interested, along with free cab rides home. On graduation night, we implemented a mandatory breathalyzer test for everyone who left the building. Fail the test, no keys. Although it was harsh, the program received immediate recognition from both local and national news channels. For my participation, I was named Minnesota's Outstanding High School Senior for 2010 and was later elected as a Rising Star within the national chapter of SADD.

Although Joshua occasionally teases me about my vigilance, he respects my position on the issue. I also suspect that I am a good influence on him, because he is now a regular participant at SADD meetings. I hate the thought that I almost lost him, but I am grateful for the new outlook that his "near miss" had on my life. Every day is a gift. Although life is filled with unavoidable problems and pitfalls, drinking doesn't have to be one of them. We all have a responsibility to make good choices. Through SADD, I am proud to do my part to help those whose momentary lapses in judgment could possibly be fatal.

Significant Awards or Honors   (400 word limit)

Konichiwa... Bonjour... Lee how ma...

My friends often speculate about why I became fluent (or semi-fluent) in five different languages. My answer: "It's my nature." Armed with an inquisitive personality, I treasure the artistic and mystical makeup of different languages, along with the benefits of learning about other cultures.

In December of 2001, New York City Mayor Rudolph Giuliani rewarded my passion by presenting me with a Citizen's Gold Star, which is a civilian's highest honor. Following the terrorist attack on the World Trade Center, I responded to an urgent call for volunteers who spoke Japanese, French, English and Vietnamese.

A rare "quadruple threat" in languages, I received permission to leave school and answer the mayor's call. For five days, I served as a translator for survivors, rescue workers and family members who were interrogated by the police and FBI. In this horrific situation, I fought valiantly to hide my emotions. Although I couldn't eliminate the terror, my ability to speak the same language as the family members seemed to bring them comfort during those bleak hours.

Ironically, my multi-lingual lifestyle also originated in fear. In September of 1995, my mother ignored my plaintive cries and forced me into a first grade classroom where I literally could not speak the language. Armed with only a few basic phrases ("sorry," "please," "hello"), I began my formal education in an English-speaking school. Although I didn't appreciate it at the time, I had a gift for languages, which ultimately became my salvation. Within a year, I became fluent in English, while maintaining my fluency in Chinese. By the time I reached high school, I was ready to embrace the French language and culture. In subsequent years, I have also studied Vietnamese and Japanese, which allow me to preserve my connection to my Asian roots.

Occasionally, I am overwhelmed by the five languages that compete for space in my brain. As I sleep, a verb that I want to conjugate in French may miraculously manifest in Japanese! Yet, despite this occasional confusion, I am motivated by the opportunities afforded to those who speak multiple languages and appreciate different cultures: the more people I meet, the larger and more satisfying my world.

Our Assessment: This essay, albeit short, explains the candidate's passion for languages, which allowed her to earn an award for her services as a translator after the 9/11 terrorist attacks. The committee was deeply impressed by her initiative in this area, which inspired her to learn additional languages on her own time. Later, as a college student, the candidate put this knowledge to use as a translator for various departments.

Significant Awards or Honors (350 word limit)

"Ehh…Jhana, you're sick. I beg you to stop, please. Don't do it to Mr. Whiskers!"

Overwhelmed by curiosity, I ignored my lab partner's plea and forced open the skull of our fetal cat. Although it wasn't part of our lab assignment, I simply had to see the cat's brain. Lacking surgical tools, I opened its skull with the strength of my hands and the persistence of my heart. After five long minutes, I exposed a mass of pink brain matter, which was spongy to the touch. Seconds later, our whole class gathered around our lab table to glimpse the horrific scene.

Needless to say, I am fascinated by science. As a young child, I took apart most of our kitchen appliances to understand how they worked, leaving a trail of knobs, screws and batteries throughout our entire house. Through my physics and math classes, I have also learned how my car engine runs and what powers my computer. I am particularly mesmerized by the human body, which is a perfect orchestration of genetics, DNA and cell functions. Despite the body's exquisite design, even a slight irregularity in any organ or system can cause a potentially life-threatening condition.

My passion for science inspired me to enter several science fairs throughout New York and Connecticut. My paper on acid rain won first place in the 2009 New York State Science Fair and placed third in the national competition. In September of 2010, I won a Westinghouse Science Award for my research on potassium deficiency in long-distance female runners. With my advisor's help, I submitted my paper for publication in *Lancet*, which is a respected British medical journal.

My goal is to pursue a career in medical research, beginning with a biochemistry degree at Cornell. With my inquisitive mind and passion for science, I will pursue my college studies with the same zeal that I brought to my high school anatomy lab. True advancements often require going the extra mile, by opening a cat's brain or resolving ambiguous data points. I am eager to accept such challenges among the talented and motivated scientific community at Cornell.

Our Assessment: The candidate used a creative opening for this essay, which summarized her many scientific awards. By demonstrating her initiative in the lab and her willingness to ask (and answer) tough questions, she won the respect of the members of the admissions committee.

Chapter 7: Unusual Questions from Specific Schools

Many colleges ask candidates to discuss their goals, personality, and hopes for the future. Sometimes, the questions are relatively straightforward (Where do you hope to be in ten years?), while other times they are more creative (Write page 217 of your autobiography). However this type of question is stated, your goal is to answer it clearly, honestly, and with the appropriate level of insight. Ideally, the information you present should complement – rather than duplicate – the material in your other essays for that school.

As always, the power is in the details. For questions about your goals, be specific. You must also be perceptive enough to match your goals with your personal and academic strengths. Whenever possible, give logical examples to support whatever adjectives you use. (If you say you're a good writer, mention a specific paper or report that proves it. Likewise, if you say that you are articulate, mention a presentation you gave that was particularly compelling.)

These questions are hard for some candidates because they ask you to talk about yourself in an unusual way. Don't be intimidated; instead, use the opportunity to sell your strengths. Convince the reader that you have a lot to offer their specific program.

The following essays vary widely in length and topic, but they all handled these questions in an extraordinary way. By design, we have grouped the essays in the following sub-categories:

Discuss Your Career Goals
Write Page 217 of Your Autobiography
What You Wish You Had Been Asked

For each essay, we have also indicated whether or not the essay was written for the Common Application or to answer a specific question for an individual college or university. (<u>Note</u>: If the essay was for a specific school, we have also indicated the specified length limit for the response.)

To protect the privacy of the writer, the names of all people, classes, schools, places, teams, activities, and companies have been changed.

Goals   (400 word limit)

As the child of an entrepreneur, I have always understood the profound way that finance governs our social, political, and economic worlds. At age ten, I helped my father run the coffee shop that he owned in downtown Seattle. Later, I trained the twelve-member crew that launched our satellite shop at the Sea-Tac Airport. By interacting with various customers, vendors, and employees, I discovered that our ability to manage money and make strategic financial decisions would ultimately determine the long-term success of our venture.

At fifteen, my father's death from cancer taught me the importance of having adequate life insurance and a clear succession plan for a business. In the absence of these necessities, our coffee shop failed, which left us without a source of income. At the time, I yearned to save the dream that my father had envisioned for our family. Yet, as a freshman in high school, I did not have the knowledge or experience to handle sophisticated financial affairs. In hindsight, I realize that there were opportunities to save the business that we had missed, such as hiring a management company or merging with a competitor. Sadly, without financial guidance, we were forced to accept government aid simply to survive.

My family's descent from success to poverty taught me a powerful lesson: without proper management, wealth can be destroyed as easily as it can be created. As I worked different jobs to support my family and pay for college, I observed the various ways that people and businesses manage their money, with varying degrees of success. My goal is to become a certified financial planner who can help individual and corporate clients achieve their financial goals. With this in mind, I plan to major in economics to learn more about the investment strategies and valuation methods that govern the financial markets. The program at the University of Pennsylvania is uniquely suited to my goals.

Ten years from now, I hope to have the knowledge and skills I will need to help my clients make informed investment decisions that will allow them to achieve their goals within their specific tolerance for risk. By doing so, I can help other families avoid the devastating setback that mine endured, because we did not understand the importance of long-term planning. An undergraduate degree in finance from the University of Pennsylvania is the next critical step on this incredible lifetime journey.

<u>Our Assessment</u>: This candidate's unique life experiences have given him keen insight into the importance of financial planning. In this essay, he clearly explains his reasons for pursuing a career in this area.

Goals   (300 word limit)

The year I turned fourteen, my father suffered a massive heart attack that nearly claimed his life. His subsequent struggle with coronary disease, including a long-awaited heart transplant, required me to care for him while my mother supported our family. For nearly three years, I helped my father manage his illness and battle several frightening infections. At first, the stress of this responsibility - and the impact on our family - seemed overwhelming to me. Eventually, however, I developed the maturity I needed to provide him with calm and loving support during a difficult time.

To learn more about my father's illness, I studied chemistry in high school and volunteered in the Emergency Room of our local hospital. I enjoyed the opportunity to care for other people who suffered from life-threatening illnesses and injuries. During my junior year of high school, my father lost his battle with coronary disease after a long and valiant fight. Although I was devastated by his death, I knew in my heart that the skills I had cultivated would never be wasted. To help other patients in similar situations, I have decided to complete my nursing degree.

Looking back, my early experiences as a caregiver helped me to develop several strengths that are essential in a health care career. At a young age, I became mature, well-organized, and able to deal with frightening situations. I also learned how to help other patients and their families survive the worst moments of their lives. By working hard in school, I maintained a high GPA and applied my training as a Nurse's Aide in several high pressure environments. My long-term goal is to obtain my certification as a Registered Nurse and devote my life to this field. Hopefully, by taking this path, I can share the lessons I learned from my father's illness with other deserving patients and their families.

<u>Our Assessment</u>: This essay is short, specific, and heartfelt. In the final paragraph, the author also explained how her unique experiences had prepared her for her chosen major. She did an exceptional job of selling her strengths within a 300 word length limit.

Goals   (400 word limit)

My long-term goal is to pursue a career in mechanical engineering, which requires a solid background in math and science. To this end, I have pursued rigorous coursework in chemistry, physics, and calculus at the high school level, which has provided me with a theoretical and practical understanding of these disciplines. Whenever possible, I use my classroom knowledge to construct unique devices that enrich and simplify my life. Thus far, I have applied the laws of physics and motion to create hunting tools for my Eagle Scout badge, such as bows and slingshots. In a similar manner, I have used scientific principles to build different types of athletic equipment, such as a handcrafted tennis racquet. Last year, I developed a creative pulley system for resistance training, which allows me to build muscle mass at home, rather than at the gym. In honor of this achievement, I received the first place award in the 2010 National Eagle Scout Association (NESA) applied physics competition, which included a $25,000 scholarship.

When I evaluated colleges, I focused on those with strong engineering programs, which would allow me to cultivate my engineering skills on a larger scale, among similarly creative students. The Mechanical Engineering department at Columbia University, which is highly ranked, incredibly diverse, with numerous areas of research, offers an excellent opportunity for me to obtain a world-class technical education. On a practical basis, it is also located in the heart of New York City, where I eventually hope to live. By completing my degree at Columbia, I can begin to build a professional network with other students, faculty, and employers in the area.

As part of my undergraduate experience, I hope to contribute to ongoing research projects in mechanical engineering, which will teach me how to turn a good idea into a marketable product or solution. I am particularly eager to work with Dr. David Doyle, who is investigating more efficient ways to extract edible oil from legumes, which is a healthy and low-cost source of human protein. By completing my education at Columbia, where my brothers are completing their doctoral degrees with Dr. Doyle, I will have a coveted chance to carry on their legacy as students and professionals. Ideally, I will also have the opportunity to enrich campus life by cultivating my own niche in the field of mechanical engineering.

<u>Our Assessment</u>: This candidate has an excellent background for a top tier engineering program, including several top awards in national competitions. He also has two brothers in the doctoral program at his chosen school, who have given him valuable information regarding research opportunities in their group. From our perspective, the author presented the information in the correct way – he sold his strengths first, followed by his desire to live in New York City. Only at the *end* of the essay did he mention his brothers and his connection to the school. By arranging the material in this manner (rather than rely upon nepotism), he won admission to the program on his own merit.

Goals   (200 word limit)

Since I was ten years old, I have dreamed of being a cardiovascular surgeon. Although my original interest was simply to "help people," I wasn't satisfied by the idea of being a stereotypical family physician. By nature, I prefer dynamic situations, in which no two days are ever alike. I also enjoy competitive and fast-paced environments that require me to think on my feet. A cardiovascular surgeon, by nature, must possess a healthy balance of decisiveness and risk tolerance to achieve the ultimate goal: saving a patient's life. I am determined to acquire the skills I will need to thrive in this profession.

The college of Arts and Sciences at Yale will bring me a step closer in fulfilling this lifelong dream. The Hughes Scholars Program and the Honors Program offered by the Biological Sciences department will provide excellent preparation for medical school. In many ways, I have been preparing for Yale my entire life. I have taken the most demanding classes at my high school, along with two courses per semester at Rutgers University. With its renowned faculty and talented student body, Yale offers solid pre-medical training in an environment of scientific excellence. I am definitely ready for the challenge!

<u>Our Assessment</u>: This candidate only had 200 words to explain his goals, which was barely enough to scratch the surface of his interest in medicine. To make best use of the space he had, he gave a general answer in the first paragraph, followed by a brief explanation of why he chose that particular school. Under the circumstances, it was the best way to demonstrate his fit for this unique program.

Goals   (500 word limit)

"You're too young. Why don't you just enjoy being your age?" Rebellious and ambitious, I started my own business just to show everyone how wrong they were. At thirteen, I sold hand-painted T-shirts from the backyard of my parents' house. A year later, I pestered my father for enough money to start a small juice bar with two friends. Smiling triumphantly, I paid him back just five months later, but the bar closed within a year. Looking back, Newton's law taught me to know better. What goes up must eventually come down. The key is to maintain a sustained upward motion.

With my strong entrepreneurial spirit, I have never been like the rest of my friends. I am always the dreamer, the inventor and the doer. I wake up in the middle of the night with earth-shattering ideas for intriguing new business concepts. With each new venture, I realize that entrepreneurs are not greedy capitalists, but agents of change. We see opportunities that others do not and we create something from nothing.

Several years ago, I decided to learn as much as I could about business by meeting every entrepreneur in my community. Whenever possible, I attend foreign investment fairs and charitable fundraisers, where I sit next to a corporate vice-president, magazine editor, or bank president. We usually have great conversations. Every successful person I have met has given me the same advice: to devour as much information as possible about my proposed ventures.

At fourteen, I made my first international relocation, when we moved from Malaysia to Brazil. Studying in a multicultural environment has dramatically broadened my personal perspective, my business contacts, and my understanding of the world economy. In four years, I have formed friendships with people from a dozen countries and formed a "San Paolo office" in my bedroom at the dorm. My management team includes a financial analyst from India, a high-tech consultant from Japan, and me, the visionary. Combining our diverse strengths, we design and sell inspirational CDs on the internet. We form a special blend that is versatile, open-minded and dynamic: traditional Confucian team spirit with Gandhian perseverance and Japanese diligence.

The unique combination of business and international studies at Harvard is an excellent fit for my talents and skills. The cross-cultural program will enable me to become a multidisciplinary problem solver and to launch my "garage company" on a global scale. In Harvard's superior learning environment, I will further develop my intellectual capabilities and entrepreneurial drive, which will allow me to add luster to the distinguished program. I am prepared to meet the challenges of Harvard and open the doors of entrepreneurial possibility.

Our Assessment: Although she doesn't mention it until the fourth paragraph, this candidate runs a multi-million dollar internet business from her dorm room in Brazil, which was the subject of her primary application essay. At a young age, she and her partners found a lucrative niche in a highly competitive business environment. By enrolling at Harvard, she hopes to further broaden her perspective and find additional opportunities to pursue. In this essay, the candidate shows the reader that she has been an entrepreneur from the time she was born – and that she takes great pride in capturing opportunities that other people miss. She was exactly the type of insightful, hard-working and risk-taking dynamo that the university was seeking.

Goals (400 word limit)

Born and raised in Dodge City, Kansas, I am a fourth-generation farmer. My family's land includes more than two thousand acres of wheat, corn and soy, and several thousand cattle. I am everything you probably think of when you envision a farm girl: fresh-scrubbed, hard working and committed to the agricultural life. But I am consciously choosing a different direction for my career, while still being true to my small-town agricultural roots. Eventually, I would like to be a veterinarian with a large animal practice.

In a world of erratic crop cycles, the lifeblood of any small farm is usually its livestock. Our farm is no exception. Over the years, I have watched my parents work around the clock to deliver a calf or treat an injured steer with hourly doses of antibiotics. To preserve these animals, which are the source of our livelihood, a reliable veterinarian is essential.

My most vivid childhood memory was waiting for our local veterinarian, Dr. Winters, to arrive at our barn to deliver emergency treatment to our extremely-pregnant cow. Molly had enjoyed a relatively stress-free pregnancy, but her labor had stopped progressing and her vital signs were becoming erratic. My mom knew that without immediate medical help, Molly and her calf might not survive. This would not only be a terrible loss for our cow, but for our farm's economic survival.

So, we waited with Molly for several hours, until we realized that her calf was in danger. Although it was the middle of the night – and zero degrees outside – I knew that Dr. Winters would answer our call and somehow save the day. He didn't let us down, and he definitely didn't let Molly down. Upon his arrival, Dr. Winters induced her labor and delivered her healthy, but always feisty daughter, Misty. Even as a ten-year-old child, I knew that the miracle he performed that night had saved both our animals and our livelihood. To me, Dr. Winters had the best of both worlds – he made a valuable contribution to farming without the responsibilities of actually owning the land.

I am excited about following in his footsteps and making veterinary science my career. I also believe that I am well-suited to it, both academically and psychologically. Ten years from now, I hope to start my own large animal practice, which will offer the same, old-fashioned, 24-hour-a-day service that Dr. Winters provides. Who knows, maybe someday, I will save the life of an injured animal and become another child's hero. It would be my highest honor.

Our Assessment: This candidate, who was extremely active in the 4-H Youth Development Organization, was well suited for any sort of agricultural career. In this essay, she explains her long-term interest in veterinary science, which offered a way for her to combine her experience in farming with her passion for animals. The essay was well perceived.

Goals (500 word limit)

"Hey, what's that thing on your back?" Ryan asked. A second later, the entire soccer team stared at the needle sticking out of my right shoulder. I quickly yanked my sweatshirt over my head as I left the locker room.

"It's for my upper back pain." I mumbled, hoping to satisfy their curiosity. No such luck.

"A pin?" Ryan looked confused.

For my entire life, I have lived in two different worlds. As a first generation Indian-American, I spend my summers in Bangalore, where I visit my extended family and embark on pilgrimages to Hindu temples. During my annual acupuncture treatments, the "pins" to which Ryan referred help to diffuse my chronic back pain from a childhood accident. My life in the United States, on the other hand, has exposed me to an entirely different culture, in which students typically seek more "traditional" therapies for their injuries. As the first Indian student to play soccer at my school, I have embraced every opportunity to bridge the two cultures. My acupuncture needles, which intrigued my American peers, are just one "exotic" aspect of my Indian heritage.

In rural Alabama, where I have spent most of my life, I have always viewed my environment as a mixed blessing. Although I greatly appreciate the small town atmosphere, our under-funded public school system lacks the unlimited resources of more wealthy suburbs, such as language labs, advanced science classes, and exposure to the arts. As a result, I must frequently utilize other avenues to enhance my educational experience. Over the years, I have become a skilled researcher who explores the vast resources of the Internet and public library system. I also view my family trips across the globe as invaluable educational opportunities.

After graduation, I am eager to immerse myself in the amazing resources that a large, diverse, world class university will afford. At the same time, I am determined to remain true to my small town roots, which acknowledge the importance of strong personal relationships. When I envision my professional future, I hope to practice medicine in a rural community, as my father has done for 23 years. My background, as a first generation Indian-American, provides a unique opportunity for me to incorporate the best aspects of Eastern and Western medicine in my future practice. Hopefully, by the time I graduate from medical school, non-invasive techniques such as acupuncture will have gained acceptance as a viable treatment for all types of illnesses and injuries. They are certainly more effective for my chronic back pain than drugs and surgery.

Many times, such as that day in the locker room with Ryan, I find myself educating others about the benefits of alternative medicine. He smiled appreciably as I explained the significance of the needle. "Interesting," he smiled. "It's a lot easier than having an operation."

As we discussed our respective health care systems, I marveled at our similarities; we were simply two intelligent young men who were exploring a chance to learn more about the world around us. With my unquenchable thirst for knowledge, I am excited about my future learning experiences in college and medical school. By challenging myself both inside and outside the classroom, I hope to explore my strengths and carve out my own unique place in the world. Hopefully, I will also help others to understand new ways of thinking and healing.

Our Assessment: This candidate used the same essay to answer questions about diversity and "why our school." By beginning with a story about his own acupuncture treatments, he tied together several themes in the same draft – his multicultural upbringing, his interest in Eastern medicine, and his desire to expand his perspective beyond the borders of a small southern town. The author conveyed a lot of information in a relatively small space.

Goals   (600 word limit)

Throughout my life, I have struggled to balance both halves of my Iraqi-American heritage, which celebrate two highly disparate political philosophies. My parents, who immigrated to the United States after surviving Desert Storm and the subsequent Iraqi military regime, refused to abandon the traditional beliefs of the oppressive government. As a result, they discouraged my interest in the humanities and social sciences, which evaluate the merits of different cultures and beliefs. Instead, they insisted that I pursue a career in a traditional field, such as law, medicine, or mathematics, which would bring honor and prestige to our family. My interest in journalism, which favors truth over stability and freedom over obedience, is impossible for my parents to comprehend.

Ironically, their stories about government secrecy and oppression catalyzed my interest in seeking the truth, regardless of how ugly or disturbing it might be. Far too often, reporters in Iraq are only allowed to publish material that the government approves. When citizens challenge that structure, the government reacts quickly and violently, such as the public violence against protestors in Fallujah and Tikrit, which left hundreds of innocent people dead and wounded. Nevertheless, for people like my parents, it is blasphemous to question the authority or motivation of the government – or the validity of the stories that are published. To me, their blind acceptance of false and misleading ideas simply perpetuates the government's tyranny.

Throughout history, American journalists have risked their lives to protect democracy by seeking and reporting the truth. Without their heroic efforts, we would never have known about Deep Throat, Watergate, the Monica Lewinski scandal, and the atrocious conduct of U.S. troops in Vietnam, Guantanamo, and Abu Ghraib. After a lifetime of seeking the truth in a household that suppresses it, I am eager to build a career that will allow me to shed light into the darkest corners of humanity. By becoming a journalist, I can join brave pioneers such as Bob Woodward and Edward R. Murrow, who ensured that our government truly represents the will of its people. Ideally, I can also inspire others to cherish the unique freedoms that American society affords.

When I evaluated prospective colleges, I focused on those with strong journalism programs and a demonstrated commitment to diversity. Northwestern University's broad and flexible curriculum will allow me to explore the historical evolution of journalism by taking classes such as Government & Media, Society & Oppression, and World Culture in the Digital Age. By studying inspirational figures such as Plato, Socrates, Einstein, and Churchill, who compelled their peers to challenge conventional wisdom and unjust authority, I hope to gain a better perspective of the impact of journalism on different people and societies.

Additionally, Medill offers unique opportunities for me to expand my skills by speaking, writing, investigating, and reporting on a variety of topics for local newspapers, radio, and television stations. With my specific interest in global affairs and my familiarity with the Iraqi language and culture, I am uniquely qualified for internships at media outlets with an international reach, such as CNN. Compared to New York City and Los Angeles, where the competition is formidable for most opportunities in journalism, Chicago offers an incomparable chance for me to gain practical experience as a reporter. By enrolling at Northwestern, I can explore the amazing possibilities the profession has to offer.

Throughout my life, I have been deeply inspired by reporters such as Walter Cronkite, David Halbertam, Peter Arnatt, and Edward R. Murrow, who risked their lives to pursue the truth and transform society in a positive way. By studying journalism at Northwestern – and by exploring the social, political, and historical roots of this distinguished profession – I can prepare for a challenging and satisfying career that will allow me to join their ranks and make a lasting contribution to global society.

Our Assessment: This essay is smart, focused, revealing and insightful. It also makes a compelling case for why the candidate chose the school he did. By including details about his own life and the journalists who inspired him, he gained a competitive edge over other candidates who spoke in generalities.

You have been asked many questions on this application, all asked by someone else. If you were in a position to ask a thought-provoking and revealing question of college applicants, what would that question be? (500 word limit)

As a seasoned bibliophile, I have discovered that the fastest route to discovering a person's character is to inquire about his reading habits. Therefore, I wish that the admissions committee had asked me to discuss my two favorite books and how they have changed my life.

On an intellectual level, I have been most challenged by *Narcissus and Goldmund* by Hermann Hesse, which I read for the first time last summer. After I put it down, I was too excited to sleep, because it forced me to explore my own preconceptions about goodness, generosity and the true meaning of life. What, for example, constitutes a successful life – is it fulfilling society's expectations or having the courage to create your own path? And who is more generous – the devoted mother who cares for her children or the childless woman who selflessly serves her community? Since these concepts are so complex, I knew that I had only begun to understand them; clearly, the book contained countless messages that I had not yet grasped from my initial reading. Unlike most works of fiction, with *Narcissus and Goldmund*, I had a book that I would re-read multiples times in order to gain additional insight into Hesse's underlying messages. Ideally, I could also use that information to become a more insightful and sensitive person in an increasingly insensitive world.

In contrast, *Black Like Me* moved me emotionally by the explicit way it depicted the cruel racial taunts the author endured. As a white woman, I was moved to tears by his description of the differences in people's responses to him, depending on whether he presented himself as black or white. Sadly, the author's occupation, clothing, wealth, speech, and identity were irrelevant when his skin was black. As a racial minority, he was considered to be worthless and unwanted, a drain on society. Because this book was non-fiction, my reaction was particularly strong; these people were real, as was their hatred. *Black Like Me* forced me to take a stand on racism, including the subtle ways it exists in my own community. After reading the book, I took the initiative to promote equality on the Math Team and Pep Squad, where I am a trainer and judge. Whenever possible, I make my selections based on performance rather than preconceptions. I also hold open-door meetings to encourage minority students to join the fun.

Unlike most bibliophiles, I do not expect my books to provide the final answer for everything. Instead, I prefer to apply the information I gain to situations in my own life, hopefully with a broader and more knowledgeable perspective. In this respect, books are not just a source of entertainment, but a way to explore new places, ideas and opportunities from the comfort of my bedroom. The greatest books, such as *Narcissus and Goldmund* and *Black Like Me*, are my favorites because they helped me to learn more about myself.

<u>Our Assessment</u>: This essay was successful because it was the only place in the application that the candidate actually talked about herself. In every other essay, she played it safe by choosing neutral topics, such as a need for funding for the arts. This essay about her favorite books gave the committee a better feel for who she was as a person – and what mattered most to her.

You have been asked many questions on this application, all asked by someone else. If you were in a position to ask a thought-provoking and revealing question of college applicants, what would that question be? (500 word limit)

What was the greatest meal you have ever eaten?

In my family, there is nothing better than a good "home-cooked" Italian meal. My most memorable dinner was two years ago in Italy, at the home of my maternal grandmother. Despite the oppressive heat and humidity, Grandmother Morelli was determined to prepare a feast that was worthy of her visiting granddaughter. Using only organic ingredients from the local market, she spent hours in her tiny kitchen preparing ravioli, salad, and fresh garlic bread.

As the guest of honor, I was not expected to help in the kitchen. Nevertheless, I was eager to stir the pot and possibly pick up a few cooking tips. For over an hour, my grandmother and I worked silently in the tiny galley kitchen, chopping, boiling and sifting a seemingly endless supply of ingredients. Finally, we reached a lull when the hard work was done; our salads awaited tossing, while the ravioli and garlic bread baked slowly in the oven.

To my surprise, rather than take a break, my sweet grandmother started to cry. At first I was nervous, then somewhat embarrassed. I wondered if I had done something wrong. Her emotional hug gave me my answer, along with an unexpected lesson in family history. It seems that my afternoon in the kitchen was actually a family tradition that dated back nearly a century. My grandmother had learned to cook in that very room, and later took great pride in teaching my mother how to prepare the same dishes. In her mind, by learning how to make the Morelli specialties from scratch, I would be able to pass down the same tradition to my own children some day.

On an intellectual level, it made no sense, because having children was the furthest thing from my mind. Yet I instinctively knew that the occasion was not about logic, but the deep emotional connection between the two of us. In a split second, I understood the importance of family and history. Although my mother had told me dozens of stories about growing up in Italy, I could never relate to them. In a million different ways, her childhood in Verona was completely different from my own experiences in the heart of Manhattan. Yet, despite our differences, we now shared the ritual of cooking a special meal for our hungry family. I was honored to be part of something so special.

Looking back, neither my grandmother nor I was the greatest cook that night; the ravioli was overcooked and the garlic bread was soggy. But, miraculously, no one seemed to notice. For several hours, my large extended family ate, drank, and laughed through dozens of stories about events from long ago. Sometimes, when she was really excited, my grandmother began to speak in broken Italian, which no one could understand. And it really didn't matter. That meal, surrounded by the members of my mother's family, remains a cherished moment in my life. As I plan my future, I am eager to take additional trips to Verona, to explore the people and places that my extended family calls home.

<u>Our Assessment</u>: This is a lovely essay about a cherished family memory that the candidate enjoyed on her trip to Italy. It gave the committee a glimpse into her personal background that was not covered anywhere else on her application.

You have been asked many questions on this application, all asked by someone else. If you were in a position to ask a thought-provoking and revealing question of college applicants, what would that question be? (300 word limit)

I would ask the applicants to identify and explain their greatest passion. In my case, the answer would be Bharat Natyam, the Indian Classical dance that I have studied for the past three years. At this point, I am still very much a novice, as Bharat Natyam requires seven years of dedication, discipline and commitment to fully perfect the technique. Each hand gesture, facial expression and eye movement tells a specific part of the story. In addition to the graceful execution of each move, classical dance also requires an understanding of its cultural meaning. My training requires an integration of numerous technical skills and a heartfelt dedication that can only come from the soul.

The discipline I have developed from studying Bharat Natyam has had many benefits in my academic career. Over the past three years, I have developed the intense concentration that is appropriate for each movement. I have also learned how to open my heart, which enables me to connect with the dance on a deeper spiritual level. When I am disappointed by my progress, I am inspired by my teacher, who has studied classical dance for more than 30 years. I watch how each basic step, which is frustrating to perfect, emerges over time into a beautiful sequence that tells a story. Yet I also know that she mastered the dance just like me, with attention and dedication, over a long period of time. Building my career will also be a step-by-step process, which will require me to complete my education, select a career path, and learn the intricate details of my chosen profession. Although I have not yet begun to cultivate the skills I will need to succeed, through Bharat Natyam, I have already developed the heart and soul of a leader.

<u>Our Assessment</u>: This essay is short, concise, and surprisingly moving, because it explains what Bharat Natyam means to the candidate on an emotional basis. The committee was highly impressed by the commitment and discipline that she had cultivated to perfect this difficult dance.

You have been asked many questions on this application, all asked by someone else. If you were in a position to ask a thought-provoking and revealing question of college applicants, what would that question be? (Common Application: 750 word limit)

What do your possessions say about you?

A recent survey in *Cosmopolitan* magazine tried to predict the reader's personality from the contents of her bedroom. After taking the quiz, which missed the mark more often than it hit it, I wondered what a total stranger would think when he or she entered my room. What would my possessions convey about my personality, interests, and character?

Upon entering, a visitor would first notice the absence of posters, knickknacks and trophies that cover the walls of most teenagers' bedrooms. In my case, the lack of adornment is a simple preference for clean walls, which provide a sense of tranquility. Ironically, my zen for cleanliness does not extend to the rest of the room, where the bed lies unmade and yesterday's wardrobe gathers dust on the floor. I hope that the visitor's first impression would be that I am tidy, but not inflexible.

While touring the room, the most impressive feature is my workspace, desk and computer, which are neat, well-used and well-organized. My desktop includes the typical pencil holder, books and desk calendar, which is filled with important dates: tests, deadlines, and an occasional day off from school. My non-academic interests are reflected by the top of my bureau, which is covered by several personal items, including a postcard from my best friend, a present from my grandfather, and my uniform from my job at Chick-Fil-A. The postcard reveals my spiritual side, as it includes a famous quote by Mahatma Gandhi about the importance of maintaining peace in one's soul. Although I have never visited India, I am intrigued by its religion and culture, which play a fundamental role in my best friend's life.

On my nightstand are two stacks of books, including a healthy balance between school texts and carefully selected items for pleasure reading. I hope that my visitor would interpret their presence as evidence of my desire to be well-read on both an intellectual and recreational level. The presence of two daily newspapers, *USA Today* and the *Miami Herald*, confirms my desire to stay abreast of what is going on in the world.

Although my mother disapproves, I consider my perpetually unmade bed as a symbol of rest and quietude. On an aesthetic level, the plaid comforter and mismatched sheets do not reflect my personal style as much as my laziness on cleaning day. Since my bedroom is my haven, my bed would be precious to me regardless of how I chose to "gussy it up." To me, it is perfect just the way it is. After all, it is where I read, study, and talk on the phone. It's where I watch TV, paint my nails, and prepare for oral book reports. It's even where I "veg out" when I need a short break from the rat race. In hindsight, some of my best moments have occurred while lying on the bed and staring at the ceiling, pondering the nature of relationships, college and careers.

The final item in my room is the requisite stereo system and assorted collection of tapes and CDs. Upon perusing my selection, a visitor would rightfully conclude that my musical taste is eclectic, but leans heavily toward classic rock. Past the techno-tunes of the Eighties lie my current favorites in alternative rock, along with a sprinkling of country, classical and jazz. Regardless of my mood, these sounds provide a sense of tranquility while I am doing homework, writing reports, or completing my college applications. They hopefully show my non-academic side, which gives me a breather from the more rigorous aspects of life.

After exiting my room, I would hope that my visitor would conclude that I am a happy, healthy, well-adjusted girl who loves to learn new things. Blessed with a passion for music, philosophy and world events, I am the typical girl next store who hopes to pursue a satisfying career as a teacher. Rather than seeing my lack of cleanliness as a flaw, I hope they would see it as a quaint eccentricity, which builds character. After all, if a little dirt is the most embarrassing thing in my room, I would easily pass the inspection of whatever visitor might drop by.

Our Assessment: This clever essay introduces us to the candidate by describing the items in her bedroom. By explaining the significance of each – and keeping the discussion serious yet lighthearted – the author proves that she is smart, insightful, with a wide range of hobbies and interests. She also knows who she is and what she wants to accomplish in life, which impressed the schools that accepted her.

Write page 217 of your 300-page autobiography. (500 word limit)

In my native Greece, the slogan "Faster! Higher! Stronger!" is written on the walls of the three gymnasiums where I train in martial arts. For more than ten years, as I practiced each day, those principles became deeply embedded in my mind and heart. As a result, I always believe I can improve my performance and achieve greater feats, regardless of the praise I receive from others.

Unfortunately, my faith in these principles eventually led to a grave misfortune in my athletic career. In 2024, after winning three consecutive Olympic Gold Medals for my homeland, I considered myself to be in peak athletic form. In a sport that is dominated by teenagers, I somehow managed to retain the poise, stamina, and concentration of competitors half my age. In addition to teaching and coaching martial arts, I was a fearless gymnast who refused to accept the limitations of middle age. Sadly, fate had other plans for me.

To prepare for the 2024 Olympics, I embarked on a grueling eighteen-day training regimen. In my quest to qualify, I over-trained and acquired Osgood-Schlatter Disease, which is one of the most common causes of excruciating knee pain among professional athletes. My doctor gave me an unenviable choice: to quit martial arts or to continue competing and suffer the consequences of becoming physically handicapped. It was a tough decision. Fortunately, I was mature enough to quit.

At the time, it seemed like the end of my world. Eventually, however, I gained considerable comfort from the lessons my career had given me. As an athlete, I had learned the art of perfection, how to endure fatigue and pain, how to harness my fears, control my mind, body and spirit, and, finally, how to win and lose gracefully. If not for these skills, I would never have acquired the gold medals, the prestigious coaching position or partial ownership in the gymnasium. I would not have been invited to give inspirational speeches to budding athletes across the globe. Although the end of my martial arts career was an unexpected transition, I walked away with a powerful sense of optimism for the future.

Our Assessment: Many candidates hate this question because they do not know how to answer it. In this case, the candidate simply fantasized about the person he hoped to be in 2024, which was an Olympic athlete at the top of his game, until a devastating diagnosis ended his career. The resulting essay is powerful and well written. It was well perceived.

Write page 217 of your 300-page autobiography. (500 word limit)

Surprisingly, by age 40, my lucrative business had lost its allure. After a few tense talks with my husband Jeff, I opted to sell my thriving internet business to my assistant, who was still in love with the e-commerce rat race. With over a million dollars in my pocket, I moved to Key West, where "Embrace Margaritaville" was the city motto.

My cozy beach house was the perfect place for me to collect my thoughts and ponder the next stage of my career. As I watched the sun disappear into the horizon, I realized how truly happy I was. Once again, I felt the thrill of new beginnings and the excitement of things to come. Jeff, on the other hand, missed the excitement of the mainland and channeled his restlessness into various home improvement projects. Less than a month after our arrival, he insisted on converting our tiny garage into a home-based office. The resulting "oasis," which was fully-equipped with the latest communication technology, enabled him to juggle his work with family time, which was our reluctant compromise. Even in paradise, Jeff frequently worked from dusk until dawn. With our children away at school, I had hoped for more fun times in the Keys before we embarked on our annual vacation to New York. Although Jeff insisted on bringing his video-phone on the trip, he promised to keep the business calls to a minimum.

Our first days in the Big Apple were magical; I marveled at the Statue of Liberty's third renovation and caught the Andrew Lloyd Webber revival on Broadway. Jeff and I spent seven glorious days in Manhattan, where we took in every last drop of culture, shopping and music. Our next stop was Syracuse, where we stayed with my old college roommate at her recently-expanded dairy farm. For three days, we reminisced about old times with Melanie and her husband, as we gorged ourselves on fresh rolls, sweet creamery butter and hand-raised chickens from the farm. How wonderful it was to finally escape the demands of the business world!

Alas, it was not meant to be. On our last day in Syracuse, Melanie took me aside and asked me to evaluate her business plan for a potential internet enterprise. She apologized profusely for bothering me, claiming to understand my reluctance to "talk shop," but she simply knew that this was the right opportunity for us. Arrgh!

<u>Our Assessment</u>: The details in this essay are amazing to us, because they give the reader a full picture of the candidate's personal and professional status at a specific moment in time. She clearly sees herself as a successful entrepreneur who yearns to cash out and relax with her husband on the beach. The surprise ending also reveals that the candidate cannot escape her role as an entrepreneur for any length of time. The reader knows that her friend's business plan will be something that she simply can't turn down.

Write page 217 of your 300-page autobiography. (500 word limit)

Thanks to my trusty four-wheel drive, I was the only doctor on staff on the night that Hurricane Alberto hit the coast of Maine. In addition to the accident victims already in the ER, my primary concern was Ella, a kindhearted elderly woman in the final days of cancer.

Just as I was about to leave her room, I was startled by the sound of her monitor. As it blared its intimidating "beep, beep, beep," I took a closer look at the frail, white-haired woman attached to miles of tubing. Why did this have to happen now? She was resting so comfortably. Was it possible that her body simply didn't want to deal with the burgeoning storm?

Glancing at her hands made me reminisce about the many years that Ella had been my patient. Hands that had rocked tiny babies to sleep and fed them their carefully warmed formula. Hands that created vibrant party dresses, aprons, and blouses for her fashion-conscious daughters. Hands that had come together in prayer at the news that the "small spot" on her lung wasn't as innocuous as we had originally hoped. How many times had I held those hands and chatted with her about topics big and small? As I glanced at the ring on Ella's finger, I thought of her late husband Harold, who was undoubtedly waiting for her in heaven. Would their long-awaited reunion be tonight? Not if I could help it.

In the past year, I often saw the frightened child in Ella, who was simply not ready to die. With six adult children and eighteen grandchildren nearly, Ella still had much to live for. Although her nauseating cancer treatments were a startling contrast to how she had planned to live out her final days, she endured them with dignity. She wanted as much time on earth as I could possibly give her.

Looking at her face, I noticed her resemblance to my own mother, who had died the previous November. I knew the pain that Ella's children would go through if I couldn't revive her. Losing a mother is one of the greatest pains in the world, a knife wound to the heart. I hoped to delay that pain for the Alvarez family for at least another day.

Reaching out to touch Ella's hand, I quietly rejoiced when I felt her faint pulse. "False alarm," I called to the frantic nurse. "She's going to be just fine."

Our Assessment: In his primary statement, this candidate discussed his interest in becoming a physician. This essay gives the reader an excellent feel for the empathy and compassion he will bring to the job. The focus, detail, and tone are extraordinary.

Write page 217 of your 300-page autobiography. (300 word limit)

On our long-awaited second honeymoon, Kyle and I spent a leisurely week exploring San Jose, Costa Rica, a city renowned for its historic museums, shopping opportunities, and exquisite cuisine. We had planned to take the trip a decade earlier, but we were forced to cancel it when I was diagnosed with colon cancer. After surviving the grueling regimen of chemotherapy and radiation, followed by reconstructive surgery, I considered the trip a much-deserved reward for cheating death.

For breakfast, we enjoyed sesame bread, feta cheese, rose jam and tea at an open-air market and café. As we ate, we absorbed the breathtaking scenery of the Central Valley, which separates San Jose from Costa Rica's other primary cities. Although it is now a tourist district, the narrow streets, old shops and distinct architecture provided us with a rare glimpse of centuries past.

Afterwards, we visited the National Theater and Lankester Botanical Garden, whose lush greenery literally took our breath away. Then, we enjoyed a concert at the Melico Salazar Theatre, where my parents first met more than seventy years ago. After sharing my wonderful memories with Kyle, we took several photos to share with our daughter Dolores. We later made our way to the Gold Museum, where we bought souvenirs for our friends and family.

For lunch, we visited a seaside bakery that offered delicious fruit pastries and scones. We took our seats on the oceanfront courtyard, where the diners are frequently splashed with sea water. For an afternoon jaunt, we explored the San Jose Bazaar, where more than one thousand shops sell spices, carpets, jewelry and leather goods. We finished our fulfilling day at an upscale seafood restaurant, followed by a quiet walk back to our hotel. Gazing into the night sky, I pondered the Costa Rica of centuries ago, before the influx of tourists, when San Jose was a very different place.

Our Assessment: This author struggled with this topic, because she had no definitive idea of where she hoped to be in twenty years. Instead, she thought about all of the wonderful things she experiences on her recent trip with her family to Costa Rica. Then, with a few changes (such as adding a husband and projecting the events into the future), she presented that trip as the topic of this essay. For candidates who are struggling with this type of question, it is a viable approach.

Chapter 8: Older & Nontraditional Students

Although most college applicants are recent high school graduates, some are significantly older than their peers and have several years of work experience. For these candidates, the application essay is a golden opportunity to update the committee on what you have accomplished since you graduated from high school. Ideally, your essay should also explain the type and extent of your professional experiences and how they have influenced your goals.

Here are several excellent essays from older and non-traditional candidates who gained admission to highly competitive programs. For each essay, we have also indicated whether or not the essay was written for the Common Application or to answer a specific question for an individual college or university. (Note: If the essay was for a specific school, we have also indicated the specified length limit for the response.)

To protect the privacy of the writer, the names of all people, classes, schools, places, teams, activities, and companies have been changed.

Older and Nontraditional Students   (Common Application: 750 word limit)

As children, my siblings and I loved to play in an abandoned field in our neighborhood in Sao Paolo. One day, my brother fell into a hole while he was running across the field. When I heard his cries, I raced to the spot and immediately tried to free his foot, which was sliced by jagged pieces of metal. Instinctively, I pulled him to safety and made a "medicinal" concoction from the leaves of a nearby tree. In subsequent weeks, as my brother recovered, he began to call me a curandera, or healer.

At age five, I was honored – and humbled - by this title, which held considerable reverence and affection in Brazilian society. Although I was not familiar with the curanderas' rituals, I shared their desire to help people eliminate pain and suffering. By pursuing a medical career, I hoped to use my natural talents to provide compassionate care to the people who needed it the most. Ideally, I could also assume a nurturing and educational role in my community.

At age eight, I accompanied my family to the United States and began to assimilate into American culture. By mastering English and excelling in my classes at a public school in Miami, I achieved a significant personal milestone – I became the first person in my family to graduate from high school. Unfortunately, on a financial basis, my parents could not afford to send me to college, which was an integral part of my professional plans. Nevertheless, as the oldest of eight siblings, I was determined to set a positive example by continuing my education.

A job at Miami-Dade General Hospital offered the perfect solution. First, through the employee benefits program, I took several college classes for free. Second, as an employee of a prestigious teaching hospital, I had the chance to work in a fast-paced medical setting and observe the interactions of the health care team. More than ever, as I worked with patients and their families, I was drawn to a career in medicine.

On 9/11, the terrorist attack on the World Trade Center forced me to re-evaluate my plans. In an instant, my desire to serve society assumed a new sense of urgency. A month later, I enlisted in the U.S. Army and completed the training to become a radiologic technologist. The military was an eye opening experience for me, which revealed a level of strength and resilience that I didn't know I had. By drawing upon the solid values my parents instilled in me, I became a disciplined leader with the confidence to lead others, complete missions, and accept higher responsibilities.

Not surprisingly, my work as a radiological technologist has also offered unique rewards and challenges. In the past seven years, I have been privileged to work with a broad spectrum of patients in numerous emergency departments, intensive care units, step down wards, and rehabilitation facilities. As a Second Lieutenant in the Medical Services Corps, I am currently working with soldiers and civilians in the Surgical ICU at Walter Reed Army Medical Center. This position has given me a rare opportunity to treat patients who have incurred devastating wartime injuries. As part of a dedicated health care team, I have gained the trust and confidence of many patients, family members, and mentors. I have also had the chance to work with several accomplished physicians who use their skills to improve the quality of people's lives. Their courage and dedication during difficult times has given me a powerful example to emulate.

At family gatherings, my brother always mentions that life-changing moment when I pulled him from the hole and treated the wound on his foot. More than thirty years later, the spirit of a curandera continues to guide my life. Yet, from a practical perspective, I have much more to contribute to the medical profession besides my youthful idealism. My unique experiences as a soldier and health care worker have transformed me into a confident person with a passion to make a difference. Most importantly, they have ignited my desire to improve society by eliminating people's pain and suffering. After a lifetime of preparation, I am ready to embrace the challenges that a pre-medical curriculum to present. I am ready to become a doctor.

Our Assessment: This is a powerful essay from a driven and accomplished candidate. After challenging herself in the military, she had a clear understanding of who she was, what she wanted, and what was required to get there.

Older and Nontraditional Students   (250 word limit)

Challenges are a part of life; how we handle them ultimately defines our character. During my junior year of high school, I endured two major crises—the loss of my mother to cancer (which signified the end of my past), and the loss of our family home to foreclosure (which signified a sad and uncertain future). Taken alone, each of these challenges would have been difficult. Together, they provided a devastating blow. For several months, I grieved the loss of my mother as I packed her belongings and moved into my grandmother's home. Every item that I handled reinforced my feelings of sadness and isolation. Throughout my high school years, my mother's greatest wish was for me to attend Yale University, which had been her alma mater. Sadly, neither she nor I had the chance to see my dream become a reality.

Despite these setbacks, I refused to accept defeat. With the encouragement of my friends and family, I returned to St. Mary's High School and graduated with honors. With the support of my English teacher, I published a book of poetry through Random House and accepted a position as a junior editor in their New York office. In the past two years, my supervisor Diane Landry has been an inspirational mentor and role model for me. With her support, I have revived my plans to enroll in the creative writing program at Yale and pursue my educational dreams.

In my free time, I continue to make a positive impact in my community. Recently, I led a fundraiser for the Wyoming Hospice Association, which serves the needs of cancer patients and their families. I am also a "friendly visitor" for their volunteer program, which has allowed me to flex my skills as a caregiver. By facing my challenges with optimism and perseverance – and by sharing my experience with other cancer patients and survivors - I have become a stronger person who can empathize with the plight of others. Most importantly, I have comforted other friends and family members who have survived the loss of a loved one to this dreadful disease.

Our Assessment: This is a lovely essay about a difficult loss that changed the candidate's life. Rather than dwell on the negative, she explains the many things she has accomplished since then, which have given her the confidence to pursue her educational dreams. The candidate used the same essay to answer a question about a difficult obstacle she had overcome. It was well perceived.

Older and Nontraditional Students (Common Application: 750 word limit)

For most of my childhood, I cringed in fear whenever I opened our front door. My mother's boyfriend, who shared her addiction to alcohol, brought additional stress into our already troubled home. On any given day, I never knew if there would be food in the house, a visit from the police, or if my mother would be sober. Despite this trauma, I struggled to complete my education and be a positive role model for my younger sister. Unfortunately, an unplanned pregnancy at age sixteen threatened to disrupt my plans.

In an instant, I found myself with a level of responsibility for which I was completely unprepared. When I moved to a shelter in search of support, I was forced to drop out of school and abandon my quest for an education. My daughter's birth, followed by my efforts to obtain my GED and work a full-time job, provided a powerful epiphany about my long-term goals. Without the benefits of an education, I could not provide my daughter with the safe and successful life that she rightfully deserved. Even worse, I felt trapped by the negative stereotype of early parenthood, which prevented people from taking my ambitions seriously. To escape the poverty, neglect, and abuse that had ruined my own childhood, I made a bold choice: I resigned from my job as a waitress and enlisted in the United States Air Force.

From this start, this decision proved to be the right one; the structure and rigor of the military was an excellent match for my driven personality. Through dedication and commitment, I survived the challenges of basic training and graduated at the top of my class. Within two years, I was promoted three pay grades and received several awards, including Airman of the Year. My deployments to places as diverse as Costa Rica, Japan, and various locations in Africa not only allowed me to see the world, but to pursue my love of languages, which had been my favorite activity in high school. By accepting the challenges the Air Force presented me, I finally escaped the disappointment and low expectations that had haunted me as an unmarried teenage mother.

Ironically, when I reflect upon the troubles in my past, I am haunted by a sad realization – that I am one of the "lucky" ones. Across the country, there are millions of abused and neglected children who pay a terrible price for their parents' poor decisions. Without the support of a devoted mentor and role model (or the benefits of an education), they have little opportunity to build a better future. Far too often, they succumb to the temptations on the street, such as drugs, sex, gangs, and violence, which destroy their chances for success and independence. As someone who has beaten the odds, I am determined to be part of the solution.

By completing my degree and pursuing a legal career, I hope to acquire the knowledge and skills I will need to serve as an advocate for poor, abused, and neglected children, who require intervention and support in order to fulfill their highest potential. Eventually, I hope to draft legislation that protects their rights and gives their parents the tools they will need to be effective role models. On a personal basis, I also hope to serve as a positive example for other young women who face the challenge of early motherhood.

After coming so far, I would be honored to share the benefits of my knowledge, experience, and education with other at-risk children. By sharing my story, I hope to offer inspiration and direction to them during a particularly frightening time. Ideally, I can also convince them that their troubles at home do not have to limit or define their goals for the future. My personal transformation from single mother to successful Airman and Ivy League candidate confirms a powerful truth: with determination and tenacity, all things are possible.

Our Assessment: This is a strong essay from an incredibly strong woman. Her success in the military, combined with her volunteer work with at-risk children, is a testament to her character and determination. The candidate used the same essay to answer a question about her long-term goals. After reading it, the committee knew that she would be a tremendous asset to their school – and to the legal profession.

Transfer Student   (500 word limit)

Throughout my life, I have been inspired by the words of Albert Einstein, who advised his peers to "Learn from yesterday, live for today, hope for tomorrow. The important thing is not to stop questioning." When I arrived at the University of Wisconsin, I was determined to take this advice and find the answers to philosophical questions about the world around me. Through courses in history, politics, and languages, I hoped to become a more insightful person with the confidence to pursue my dreams. Ideally, I also hoped to interact with people from different backgrounds and cultures, who would expand my perspective on various political and social issues. In my mind, my $50,000 scholarship from the American Society of Engineering was a ticket to a life-changing educational journey.

Unfortunately, I soon discovered that declaring a major in engineering would limit my ability to explore my interests in other fields. Instead, I would need to follow a strict mathematics and science curriculum, with few elective courses. Additionally, I recognized that the educational environment at the University of Wisconsin, which offers little opportunity for professor-student interaction, was a poor fit for my personal learning style. To fulfill my goals, I needed a smaller school that encourages a lively exchange of views, both inside and outside the classroom. By the end of my first semester, I realized that I needed to change universities in order to enjoy the rewarding journey of discovery, refection, and growth that a college education should provide.

On a personal basis, I have also concluded that there are other professions that interest me beyond the realm of engineering, which I had not considered before I enrolled at the University of Wisconsin. As part of my educational experience, I am eager to explore those options among a like-minded group of professors and peers. By transferring to Brown, I can pursue a rigorous liberal arts education that will hone my strengths as a speaker, writer, and analytical thinker. I will also have the opportunity to interact with other students who share my interest in math and science. In this close-knit environment, which supports numerous research and international initiatives, I can determine the career path that will make the best use of my talents and skills. After graduation, I may join the Peace Corps and teach biology in a third world country. Alternatively, I may pursue a doctoral project to develop safer pesticides for domestic fruits and vegetables. Or, I may continue my research on fractals under the direction of Dr. Joseph Fields, who is a noted expert in the field. By completing my education at Brown, I will acquire the maturity and perspective I will need to fulfill my highest potential as a person, student, and professional. No other school offers a comparable chance for me to challenge myself academically, serve my community, and find the answers to life's biggest questions.

Our Assessment: Every year, thousands of students seek a transfer to another college or university, where they hope to achieve their educational objectives. In their essays, they must explain the reason for this change in an honest and compelling manner. In this case, the candidate was thrilled to accept a large scholarship award from a distinguished engineering group, which would pay for the full cost of his college education. Unfortunately, he soon realized that he had made a mistake by: (1) attending a large state university; and (2) declaring an engineering major, which would severely limit the range of courses that he could take. By explaining that honestly and succinctly – and by citing the specific benefits that the new university would offer him – he made a positive impression on the committee.

Chapter 9: Addendums to Explain Unusual Situations

Ideally, in a perfect world, your grades and test scores will be an excellent fit for the school that you hope to attend. But what if they aren't? Many times, as part of their applications, candidates will attach a separate addendum to explain a disappointing grade or SAT score. Their hope is that the explanation will compensate for a less than stellar "number" on their application. From our experience, these addendums rarely make a positive impact on the admissions committee.

Why? Most explanations are highly personal and difficult to verify. Other times, the excuse raises more questions than it actually answers, such as an announcement that the candidate does not perform well on standardized tests. Well, most top universities require candidates to pass dozens of timed tests in a highly competitive environment; if you cannot handle the SAT, which is the only "constant" in the application process, how do you plan to succeed in college? (I've yet to hear a persuasive answer to that question.)

Nevertheless, if you have a disappointing grade or SAT score – and a legitimate explanation for it – you should definitely explain the situation to the admissions committee in the form of a short (250 words or less), well-written addendum. If possible, you should also have an objective third party (who has no vested interest in the admissions decision) document the situation in a persuasive recommendation letter.

What are legitimate explanations?

• Medical emergencies that can be documented by a physician's letter
• A serious illness or death in the immediate family
• Military commitments/relocations
• Work commitments necessitated by financial emergencies
• Your native language is not English
• You have a documented learning disability, but did not request special accommodations for the SAT

In these cases, a well-written addendum that informs the committee of the situation (without making excuses) can greatly enhance your application. At the very least, it will give the reader some insight into the problems you have faced to complete your education and pursue your professional goals. This chapter contains several essays that candidates submitted to explain a disappointing GPA or SAT scores. To protect the privacy of the applicant, the names of all people, classes, schools, places, and companies have been changed.

Addendum to Explain Bad Grades (Transfer Student)

Although my recent academic performance is excellent, I wasn't always able to devote my complete energy to my school work. I was enrolled in the American International University during the collapse of the Colombian government, when the country underwent unprecedented economic turmoil and uncertainty. In a short period of time, my country experienced hyperinflation, rampant unemployment and a dramatic increase in violent crime. My family and I lost our life savings, including our family business. As a result, I found myself struggling to survive, rather than focusing on school.

Looking back, I am proud that I was able to balance my schoolwork with a full-time job at a restaurant. I did everything possible to ensure my family's survival during an extremely difficult time. Yet the stress of the economic overhaul made it impossible for me to concentrate on my studies. Many days, rather than prepare for exams, I stood in long lines to buy food. Thus, my grades from the American International University reflect the stress of these dire circumstances, rather than my actual ability.

Fortunately, they also show that I am a survivor. During a tumultuous situation, I was forced to re-evaluate my beliefs, aspirations and plans – and I simply refused to give up. Although my grades suffered, the experience clarified my goals, challenged my organizational skills and provided the strength I needed to overcome formidable obstacles. I am a survivor. What better strengths to bring to a career in medicine?

Our Assessment: This essay is short, focused, and sincere; it also contains information that can easily be verified by third-party sources. For one of his recommendations, this candidate submitted a letter from one of his professors in Colombia, who cited his extraordinary performance under pressure. The committee realized that he was an intelligent and hardworking young man who had done his best under difficult circumstances.

Addendum to Explain Bad Grades

When evaluating my application, I hope the committee will take into consideration my difficult adjustment to the United States. I moved to San Francisco at age fifteen, not knowing a word of English. My salvation was the school's bilingual education program, where I learned how to speak and write English, in addition to perfecting my fluency in Mandarin. With the tireless support of the faculty, I plunged into my new life in America, determined to embrace the many opportunities that were unavailable in my native Beijing.

Unfortunately, the language barrier prevented me from competing successfully with other students who were native speakers of English. Although I worked incredibly hard, my grades were primarily Bs and Cs, rather than the As I desired. Fortunately, as my English improved, so did my grades. By senior year, I was in the top 10% of my class, and won first place in the Westinghouse science competition. I was also elected as captain of Barrington High School's nationally acclaimed debate team.

Throughout my life, I have become deeply appreciative of the opportunities I have reaped by living in America. Yet my struggle to perfect the English language is most certainly reflected in my grades. When evaluating my application, I hope the committee will look beyond my grade point average and consider the tremendous effort behind them. In addition to learning a new language, I adjusted to a new culture and carved out a unique set of values and goals. This maturity will make me a more competent and empathetic student and professional.

Compared to other schools, Yale University offers a solid academic reputation and a vibrant student body that celebrates cultural and socioeconomic diversity. I am eager to take my place on campus and make a positive contribution to the world. America has given me so much; I am eager to give back the fruits of my academic labor.

Our Assessment: This is a commendable essay from a candidate who had accomplished a great deal in a short period of time. By explaining the challenges she faced in a clear and sincere manner, she won the committee's full support.

Addendum to Explain Bad Grades

As the child of an American soldier and Iraqi mother, I was raised by my maternal grandparents in the harsh conditions of post-Gulf War Iraq. At age six, I was diagnosed with rheumatic fever, which required a level of medical intervention that was unavailable in Iraq. My diseased heart grew progressively worse and eventually interfered with my normal activities.

Through the assistance of Doctors without Borders, I came to the United States for medical treatment in 1998. Although the American doctors successfully replaced my mitral valve, my adjustment to the American educational system proved to be as challenging as my medical problems. In addition to my poor English skills, I was unaccustomed to learning in a classroom setting. Throughout my childhood in Iraq, I had been sporadically tutored at home, but I had never attended school. Consequently, I found the formal education system in America to be physically and emotionally overwhelming.

Fortunately, I was up to the challenge. With the help of my father's family, I hired tutors in English, math and reading and quickly raised my grades to an acceptable level. During my sophomore year in high school, I maintained a 3.5 GPA, despite serious complications with my valve replacement. After working so hard to assimilate into my new school, I refused to let anything stop me from graduating with honors.

Although my GPA isn't the best, I cannot in good conscience blame my illness. After all, the same heart condition that nearly killed me also brought me to my wonderful new life in America. Through painful experience, I have learned to accept life's blessings along with its challenges. My illness brought me closer to my father's family, who welcomed me into their lives. My illness also forced me to rely on an internal compass that I didn't know I had. I developed patience and perseverance by continuing to attend school. I became less focused on my own feelings and more appreciative of others. I also developed a tolerance for change, which, ironically, has been the one constant in my life. Although I have recovered from my disastrous childhood in Iraq, I will retain its many lessons for the rest of my life.

<u>Our Assessment</u>: This candidate used the same essay for questions about a challenge he faced and an obstacle he overcame. It also offers an honest explanation of his struggles in the classroom. To document his time off from school, the candidate also submitted a letter from the surgeon who replaced his mitral valve. As a result, the committee understood the seriousness of the candidate's illness and the length of his recovery.

Addendum to Explain Bad Grades

My GPA was nearly perfect until I suffered a severe leg injury during my junior year of high school. While driving home from my part-time job, I spun out of control on a patch of ice and injured my right leg. In that split second collision, I broke four bones and needed extensive surgery to repair them. I also needed physical therapy to rebuild the damaged tendons.

During my two months in rehab, my focus was on my own recovery rather than my schoolwork. Although I established a good rapport with my tutor, I couldn't concentrate on my assignments. During the first few weeks, I struggled with every minor detail of my hospitalization. I went from being a confident jock to a helpless patient who needed help to go to the bathroom. Thanks to the exceptional doctors, nurses and counselors on staff, I managed to get past my initial anger and complete my rehab in just nine weeks.

Unfortunately, the emotional effects of the accident lingered well into my senior year. Because of the residual damage to my leg, I could no longer play football, which had been a huge source of enjoyment and pride. My concentration deficit was also troubling. During the fall semester, I struggled with a heavy course load, including AP classes in Calculus and Chemistry. Rather than take a reduced load, I opted to simply do my best and hope that my concentration would improve. Although it eventually did, my GPA paid a heavy price. I hope the admissions committee will understand.

Two professors (Drs. Davis and Hanson), along with my rehab specialist (Dr. White), have provided reference letters to document my struggles after the accident. I offer their letters not as an excuse, but as evidence of the powerful support that I needed to regain my mobility and graduate with my class. Several friends and advisors suggested that I take a year off to fully recover. Looking back, that option probably would have enabled me to get better grades, but I am proud to be able to graduate with my class. The accident was a setback, but not a fatal one. If given a chance, I will bring my dedication and tenacity to all of my endeavors in college. I am "back in the game" and ready to show you what I can do.

<u>Our Assessment</u>: This candidate shows the reader the *right* way to document an accident that caused a drop in GPA. He told the story quickly and honestly, including his controversial decision to accelerate his workload in order to graduate with his class. Most importantly, he included letters from two physicians who documented his situation in a supportive way. As a result, the committee understood the obstacles the candidate faced to complete his classes and recover from his injuries.

Addendum to Explain a Low SAT Score

Despite my best efforts, I have been unable to achieve the exceptional SAT scores that are expected at a school of Brown's caliber. Over the Christmas holidays, I took an extensive SAT prep course, along with private tutoring sessions with a faculty member. Even with personal coaching, I have been unable to exceed a cumulative score of 1700. I am frustrated by these results, because they do not reflect the academic excellence that I have consistently displayed in the classroom.

Despite my difficulty with the SAT, I am convinced that I am an excellent candidate for your program. Over the past decade, I have developed myriad practical skills that cannot be assessed by standardized testing. I am fluent in four languages and a successful violinist in a professional orchestra. Between 2005 and 2008, I traveled all over the world with the Vienna Boys Choir. Clearly, my SAT scores do not accurately reflect my fluency in English or my proficiency in music, which is my intended major.

Although I respect your use of the SAT as a screening tool, I hope that you will consider the "full picture" of my academic, professional and cross-cultural training in making your final admissions decision. I have worked very hard to achieve aggressive professional goals, and I will bring a wealth of practical experience to the classroom. If given the opportunity, I will be a tremendous asset to Brown.

<u>Our Assessment</u>: Many students write addendums to explain a disappointing SAT score. Few have done it better than this candidate, who explained: (1) the efforts he made to obtain a top score and (2) the distinctive strengths that he would bring to campus life.

The only controversial part of the essay is his decision to mention his preparation for the SAT, which included an expensive course and one-on-one tutoring. On one hand, this clearly suggests that the candidate took the test seriously and did whatever he could to prepare for it. On the other hand, it also shows that he had significant financial resources, which some schools consider to be an unfair advantage.

Thankfully, in this case, the candidate's application was otherwise strong, which made the SAT tutoring and prep course a non-issue. But, from our perspective, this is something that candidates should consider before they disclose that they took an expensive SAT course. It definitely shows initiative, but it also shows that you have more money than other applicants (who scored well *without* an expensive course). Consequently, it may invite a level of scrutiny that you did not expect.

Addendum to Explain a Low SAT Score

Like many foreigners who were raised in the United States, I often felt like a fish out of water. My parents moved to the US when I was fifteen, which subjected me to a huge cultural change that would subsequently define my childhood. My hardest adjustments were with language. Nothing was as difficult as having to learn English with little academic support. The school department in Raleigh had no ESL facilities, so I learned English by working with an old set of Berlitz tapes. It was not easy. My initial attempts at conversation were particularly frustrating. I could visually "see" the word in my mind, but I could not verbalize it. Verb conjugation was a nightmare (sing, sang, sung) as were similar sounding words (to, two, too). Throughout high school, mastering English has been my greatest challenge.

Although I have excelled in my coursework, I still have serious difficulties with the language portion of most standardized tests. Consequently, my performance on the verbal portion of the SAT is not nearly as high as I had hoped. To compensate for this deficiency, I continue to take elective classes in speech and writing at a local community college. I also volunteer as a language tutor for new students from South America.

As a future executive, I want to express myself with confidence, both verbally and in writing. I look forward to developing these skills at Harvard, where I will embrace every opportunity to write papers and speak in front of an audience. I am certain that I will succeed. While navigating the difficult transition from Costa Rica to the US, I developed the confidence to weather even the hardest storms.

<u>Our Assessment</u>: This candidate essentially learned English on her own, which her school principal confirmed in his recommendation letter. As a result, the committee understood the terrible hurdle the candidate faced to score well on standardized tests.

Addendum to Explain a Low SAT Score

In the spring of 2009, I prepared diligently for the April SAT, knowing that the results would play a major role in determining where I would obtain my college education. After months of drills, mock tests and classroom preparation, I was ready to show the Admissions Committee what I could do with this marathon exam.

Six days before the test, I was rushed to the emergency room at Southland Community Hospital with the most excruciating pain of my life. Lab results showed an inflamed appendix that required immediate removal. Following surgery on April 1 (see attached note from my attending physician), I recovered at the hospital for three days and returned home on Thursday, April 5. Considering my four-inch incision, my doctor recommended complete bed rest for at least five weeks.

With the SAT scheduled for April 7, I found myself in an unenviable position. Although my surgery was certainly a valid reason for missing the test, the April testing date was the last one to qualify for 2009 admission. If I missed the April test, my college enrollment might be delayed by an entire year. At the time, it seemed like an eternity.

Determined to enroll in college in the fall of 2010, I refused to miss that test. Against everyone's advice, my brother drove me to the testing site on Saturday morning and waited for me nervously in the car. I could barely stand up, much less concentrate on complex reasoning problems. Yet I survived the test and even skipped my prescription painkillers that afternoon. I was hurting, exhausted and sore beyond belief, but I completed the test. My final score (1950) is respectable, but certainly not what I expected.

As I complete my application, I am fully recovered from my surgery and eager to begin my college education. Yet my low SAT score haunts me, not just because of its mediocrity, but because of the unusual circumstances that surround it. Throughout my high school career, I have worked diligently to distinguish myself as a versatile candidate who is highly suited for Harvard. My grades, work experiences and personal references all support my honorable intentions and goals. Clearly, my SAT score does not reflect my academic potential, but the extenuating circumstances I faced on the testing day. I hope the committee will consider this as a mitigating factor when they make their admissions decision.

Our Assessment: This candidate told the entire story behind his disappointing SAT score, which was supported by letters from his physicians. As a result, the committee understood that his score did not reflect his true ability to succeed in college.

Addendum to Explain a Low SAT Score

In high school, I attained a 3.9 GPA without requesting special accommodations for my learning disabilities (dyslexia and ADHD). By employing effective study techniques, I achieved excellent grades under the same testing conditions as my peers. For philosophical reasons, I chose not to inform my professors or academic advisors of my "special needs" or challenges. Instead, I opted to keep the focus on my talents, not my limitations.

Few people supported my position, including my parents and family doctor. In fact, they unanimously agreed that my efforts to compete with "normal" students were doomed to fail. As you might expect, my decision ultimately provided a wonderful sense of empowerment. By thriving academically, I confirmed my ability to succeed in difficult situations, which inspired my commitment to other aspects of personal growth. Contrary to what my high school guidance counselor told me, there isn't anything I can't do.

In the same vein, I am proud of my "average" SAT score (1500), which I also achieved without special testing accommodations. Although it may not seem particularly impressive, it proves that I can perform at parity with other candidates under extremely stressful circumstances. And to me, that is paramount. After graduation, I will be expected to demonstrate the same skills as my peers. Why not start now?

Our Assessment: For personal reasons, this candidate did not request special accommodations in the classroom or for the SAT. In this essay, he not only explains that choice, but shows the reader the confident and inspirational person that he is. The essay was well perceived.

Addendum to Explain a Low GPA

During my junior year of high school, my father lost his job as an accountant for United Airlines. Although my mother continued to work as a retail clerk, her salary was not enough to cover our basic living expenses. Within a few months, my parents depleted their savings during my father's unsuccessful job search. Without a miracle, we faced the frightening possibility of losing our family home.

Despite my heavy academic load, I accepted a position as a web designer at Brevard Community College to supplement my mother's income. Balancing a 30-hour work week with a full-time course load was a difficult challenge that left me exhausted and overwhelmed. Sadly, it also diminished my formerly perfect GPA. Despite my best efforts, I did not obtain top grades in my math and science classes, which required considerable outside preparation. On several occasions, I missed our weekly study sessions in order to work enough hours to pay our monthly bills. As a result, my greatest accomplishment is not completing my education, but keeping my family safe and united during this crisis.

My journey, although stressful, has given me the confidence and stamina to pursue my passion for engineering. After tackling this enormous responsibility in a positive manner, I am certain that I can handle the challenges that college will bring.

Our Assessment: In this short essay, the candidate proved to the committee that he was a survivor. During a tough time, he did what was necessary to help his family and complete his own education. By balancing these demands, he developed practical skills that will enhance his performance in college.

Chapter 10: A Second Chance: Responses to Waitlist Notices

Contrary to conventional wisdom, getting into an Ivy League school isn't a simple "yes or no" proposition. In reality, there are three possible responses to your application: acceptance, rejection or waitlisting. The third category is a frustrating limbo into which thousands of candidates fall each year. What does it mean if you are placed on a waitlist for an Ivy League school?

On the positive side, receiving a waitlist letter means that you have qualified for admission. The committee evaluated your application and confirmed that your background and experience are a good fit for their program. But here's where it gets sticky; although they didn't say "no" to your request for admission, they didn't say "yes," either.

Unfortunately, top schools will rarely reveal why a particular candidate is on the waitlist or what (s)he can do to improve his/her chances. Nevertheless, if you are waitlisted at your absolute first-choice school, you have nothing to lose by continuing to market yourself to the Admissions Committee. Unless the school discourages additional contact, we recommend that you take a pro-active approach. Send a letter that restates your interest in the program. Explain the unique contribution that you will make if they admit you.

Keep the letter short and sweet -- two pages maximum. Resist the urge to summarize your life history; instead, stay focused on what you have accomplished since you first applied. Also resist the urge to discuss your disappointment at not being accepted. Your tone must be upbeat and gracious.

This chapter contains two essays/letters that candidates submitted in response to being waitlisted. To protect the privacy of the applicant, the names of all people, classes, schools, places, and companies have been changed.

Response to Waitlist Notice

Please accept this letter as my heartfelt intention to remain on the waiting list for admission to Columbia University as a pre-medical major. Since I originally applied to college last summer, I have graduated from St. Mary's Academy with a perfect 4.0 GPA. In addition to my academic success, I have also devoted considerable time to several medical-related activities:

1. As a volunteer at the St. Theresa Home for the Aged, I provide care for numerous elderly residents. My favorite patient was Lia, a 103-year-old Cuban native with a winsome smile and an insatiable zeal for life. Despite chronic respiratory ailments, Lia was perpetually friendly and optimistic. She particularly loved to share memorable stories about her childhood in Havana. During her final days, after the doctors had exhausted all possible treatment options, I sat helplessly by Lia's bedside as she struggled to breathe. By providing a kind word and a comforting presence, I helped to assuage her loneliness. Lia's courageousness in the face of death taught me invaluable lessons about the resilience of the human spirit.

2. While shadowing physicians at Rhode Island Hospital, I observed angiograms and angioplasties at the cardiac catheter lab, shadowed an attending in the telemetry unit, and learned about the administration and interpretation of echocardiograms from a third-year cardiology fellow. My most memorable experience was visiting outpatients with Dr. Alicia Sone, who is an Assistant Professor of Medicine at Brown University. Her warm bedside manner and graceful handling of difficult patients taught me the importance of compassionate patient care.

3. Since August of 2009, I have served as the volunteer coordinator for the Rhode Island Women's Auxiliary at St. Mary's Academy, where I have organized membership campaigns, promotional activities and community outreach programs in the greater Providence area. In early 2010, I chaired a campus fundraiser that raised $20,000 for cancer research.

4. In December of 2009, my mother was diagnosed with multiple sclerosis, which is a progressive and debilitating neurological disorder with limited treatment options. While assisting with her care, I have learned to view a life-threatening disease from the patient's perspective. My role in my mother's treatment encompasses several diverse aspects of the health care profession; on any given day, I am a nurse, social worker, friendly visitor and neurological researcher.

My mother's disease has inspired not only my interest in genetics but my long-term goal as a physician. For my AP Biology study project, I investigated novel methods to diagnose and treat multiple sclerosis. As part of my research, I have met several patients who are struggling with the same fears and challenges as my mother. I cherish their willingness to share the most private and frightening aspects of their lives just to help my research. By facing a debilitating illness with courage and grace, they have taught me the importance of faith in medicine. Thanks to the amazing speed of medical advances, as long as there is life, there is hope.

My primary motivation to enroll at Columbia is to acquire a superior pre-medical education in an environment that supports aggressive research on multiple sclerosis and other neurological disorders. Columbia's affiliation with the National Multiple Sclerosis Treatment Center will enable me to work with Professor Roger Slade, who is currently investigating gene replacement therapy as a possible cure. Additionally, volunteering at Columbia University Medical Center will give me invaluable experience with a heterogeneous patient base that I would not otherwise encounter.

On an academic basis, I am intrigued by Columbia's outstanding research program and its commitment to exciting and unconventional teaching methods. The inclusion of innovative undergraduate electives such as humanism, ethics and preventive medicine demonstrates Columbia's commitment to cooperative learning. In such a nurturing and highly interactive environment, I will forge long-term relationships with mentors and medical practitioners who are renowned for their excellence in research, education and patient care.

As a native of New York City, I am eager to return to the area, where I will be in close proximity to the family and friends who have encouraged my ambitious goals. Thanks to their support, I feel well-prepared for the challenges of my chosen career path. After evaluating the comparative merits of other programs, I cannot imagine a better place for me than Columbia. I would be honored to accept an offer of admission.

Our Assessment: This author built a strong case for why she chose Columbia and what she would contribute to the program if she was accepted. She also took a mature and focused approach, which made a positive impression on the committee.

Response to Waitlist Notice

I was recently placed on the waitlist for Fall 2011 admission to the University of Pennsylvania. Unfortunately, because I live in Brazil, I was not able to visit the campus to meet with a member of the admissions committee. In lieu of a personal visit, I would like to present a short written summary of several recent developments that demonstrate my ability to succeed.

Aristotle taught us that the path to success involves a constant dialogue between hardship and joy, family and career. Over the past year, my experiences have confirmed his teachings. My joy and sense of accomplishment include:

1. graduating from the Intra-American High School of Brazil with a perfect 4.0 grade point average

2. continuing my work as a volunteer tutor for learning disabled children

3. winning the Miss Teenage Brazil pageant and preparing to compete for the international title of Miss Teenage Universe in July of 2011

4. receiving a Certificate of Appreciation for my fundraising efforts on behalf of Amnesty International.

In contrast, the past year has also brought great hardship, as I lost both of my parents to cancer and faced the emotional strain of losing our family home. My grief, fortunately, was abated by the love and support of my paternal grandparents, who have always encouraged me to pursue my dreams. After waiting a lifetime to attend the University of Pennsylvania, where both of my parents completed college, I am more convinced than ever that it is the right place for me.

When I look to the future, I am eager to pursue a career as an educator. As a tutor for the San Martines Elementary School, I know the difference that a loving teacher can make in the life of a poor, uneducated child. Because I am fluent in English, Spanish and Portuguese, I will be well-suited to join the University of Pennsylvania's Bilingual Tutor Program, which provides bro bono educational assistance to low income students in Philadelphia. After graduation, I hope to broaden my skills by returning to Brazil and starting a non-profit organization to support the education of street children. The undergraduate program at the University of Pennsylvania will enable me to improve the lives of countless children who would otherwise not receive an education.

Before I applied to the University of Pennsylvania, I spoke to professors Elizabeth Sterling and George Hyatt, who strongly encouraged me to apply. After working with me for several years on behalf of Amnesty International, they felt that my talents and skills were an excellent fit for your school. If admitted from the waitlist, I am certain that I can make a lasting contribution to the student body.

Our Assessment: This letter eloquently explains the many new developments in the candidate's life, along with her fervent desire to attend the University of Pennsylvania. She also explained the unique ways that she would contribute to campus life and use her degree to improve her students' lives. By telling her story in an honest and compelling way, the candidate won the support of the committee members at her first choice school, who voted unanimously to admit her.

Chapter 11: Final Thoughts

After reading this book, we hope that you feel well-prepared to write your own persuasive college admissions essays. For best results:

1. Answer the question that was asked.
2. Write naturally, but concisely.
3. Use excellent grammar and punctuation.
4. Show your real personality (let the reader get to know you).
5. Only use humor if it works.
7. Convey a positive message (avoid cynicism).
8. Use the active voice.
9. Be specific and focused / explain events whenever appropriate.
10. Revise and polish until it is perfect.

For additional help in writing and editing letters of recommendation, admissions essays, and personal statements, please visit www.ivyleagueadmission.com.

Remember: in the college admissions process, application essays can provide the committee with information about your character, motivation and goals that they could not acquire any other way. A well-crafted essay can also explain a variety of personal circumstances (and obstacles) that have affected your performance. By writing a persuasive essay, you will increase your chances of gaining admission to the college of your dreams. Don't miss this chance to claim your destiny!

Made in United States
Troutdale, OR
08/07/2023

11874019R00060